MAGIC AND GENDER IN EARLY MODERN ENGLAND

RENAISSANCE DRAMA

Dr. Shokhan Rasool Ahmed

authorHOUSE®

AuthorHouse™ UK Ltd.
1663 Liberty Drive
Bloomington, IN 47403 USA
www.authorhouse.co.uk
Phone: 0800.197.4150

Published by AuthorHouse   08/29/2014

ISBN: 978-1-4969-9049-5 (sc)
ISBN: 978-1-4969-9050-1 (e)

Any people depicted in stock imagery provided by Thinkstock are models,
and such images are being used for illustrative purposes only.
Certain stock imagery © Thinkstock.

This book is printed on acid-free paper.

Because of the dynamic nature of the Internet, any web addresses or links contained
in this book may have changed since publication and may no longer be valid. The views
expressed in this work are solely those of the author and do not necessarily reflect the
views of the publisher, and the publisher hereby disclaims any responsibility for them.

ABSTRACT

In the sixteenth and seventeenth centuries witchcraft and magic marked a turning point in English literature in general and in plays in particular. It was popular with both the elite and the general populace to believe in the power of witchcraft, and in magic and the existence of ghosts. This influenced many Jacobean dramatists such as Shakespeare, Christopher Marlowe, Thomas Middleton, John Ford, Thomas Dekker and William Rowley to base some of their characters on the idea of the village witch and the malevolent mother figure, for example in *Macbeth, Doctor Faustus, The Witch of Edmonton,* and *The Witch.* These older plays left a new generation to focus attention on how Renaissance drama deals with the issues of witchcraft in relation to gender.

This study takes a historical approach to analyze witchcraft and magic in early modern England in the Renaissance plays: *Macbeth, The Witch of Edmonton, The Witch* and *Doctor Faustus.* This study illustrates how the writers of these plays used witches and witch scenes in different ways, to highlight different historical events in early modern England. It also examines how people in the sixteenth

CONTENTS

Abstract v

Introduction: Magic and Gender in Early Modern England ix

Chapter 1   Witchcraft and Magic in Early Modern England 1
- Witches and Witchcraft.. 1
- Magic 9
- Spells against Witches: 14
- Comic Witches:.. 16
- Hecate in both Macbeth and The Witch: 17
- Other Witch Figures:.. 21

Chapter 2   Village Witch and Elite Witch............................... 27

Chapter 3   Witchcraft and Gender 45

Conclusion 69
Bibliography 73

and seventeenth centuries believed in witchcraft and magic and how witchcraft impacted on perceptions of the contemporary writers in association with gender.

In conclusion this study will highlight the fact that most of the accused witches were old women, spinsters, widows, healers, nurses and unmarried women. So the women accused of witchcraft were not merely a mirror of an age-old stereotype nor simply a result of a patriarchal society, but were being subjected to a subordinating social control of women within the reconstruction of a patriarchal society, i.e. the terrorizing and intimidation of women by those in authority in both the sixteenth and seventeenth centuries. There were also mothers who used their maternal nurturing powers malevolently against others which is seen clearly in examples of village witch discourse. This paper also reaches the conclusion that although those accused of being witches were not all mothers. In Renaissance drama witches are seen to have maternal rather than male features as the mother figure intertwines with the witch figure and this led to anxieties over the role of mother and her maternal power during that period.

INTRODUCTION: MAGIC AND GENDER IN EARLY MODERN ENGLAND

Discussions and research on witches and gender have grown increasingly common nowadays and contemporary scholars are more interested in the subject of witchcraft and especially witches and gender in early modern England in particular. This has resulted in academic institutions all over the world offering separate courses on witchcraft in all its contexts; and they have been producing interesting work on witchcraft. Furthermore other fields of academic studies are interested in writing books and articles on witchcraft for example, numerous articles including: H. W. Herrington's *"Witchcraft and Magic in the Elizabethan Drama"* and David D. Hall's *"Witchcraft and the limits of Interpretation"*, and books such as Darren Oldridge's *"The Witchcraft Reader"*, Marion Gibson's *"Early Modern Witches: Witchcraft Cases in contemporary Writing"* and Dian Purkiss's *"The Witch in History: Early modern and Twentieth century Representations"*. Sociologists, historians and the media have produced documentary films on witchcraft and the ways that people become victims of witchcraft. For example, programmes have appeared almost monthly on BBC Radio 4 with such shows as *"Beyond Belief"* and *"A History of Private Life"*, as well as many TV series and movies such as *"Sabrina The Teenage Witch"* and *"The Craft"*.

In early modern England people strongly believed in evil spirits and ghosts. By considering the historical surveys of critics, I intend to analyse the nature of the witch, male and female, in early modern England. My analysis will focus on the nature of witchcraft, i.e. the history of male and female magic in early modern England and the factors which influenced what writers include in their work regarding magic and witchcraft. I will address gender identity on this basis and explain the role of witches in association with the construction of gender. I will examine how the gender ideology of masculinity and femininity intersect in Shakespeare's plays; the factors which influenced Shakespeare's idea of the village witch and the malevolent mother figure, for example in *Macbeth* but also considering these other plays: Christopher Marlowe's *Dr. Faustus*, Thomas Middleton's *The Witch* and *The witch of Edmonton* by John Ford, Thomas Dekker and William Rowley. This leads to a focus on how Renaissance drama deals with contemporary issues of witchcraft. I will answer these questions according to my understanding about the world of witches and witchcraft with particular reference to early modern England. How did females use their maternal power in early modern England to achieve their political goals? How was witchcraft used as an element to explore ideas of power and gender in early modern England? In terms of gender representations and sexual ambiguity, how can the mother's roles be seen in the perpetuation of patrilineage, in Renaissance drama? How is male magic portrayed in Renaissance drama?

In early modern England cunning men and women (often older people on the fringe of society) became easy targets for gossip within rural communities and the world of witchcraft was mysterious and dangerous: the subject of witchcraft was taken seriously. I will examine the perception of the mother figure in this period and how she appears in different guises: e.g. Mothers who have used their nurturing maternal power malevolently against others which is apparent in village witch discourse. I will examine the malevolent mother figure in *Macbeth* who uses her maternal power to suckle and nourish small demons as though they were children. After exploring witchcraft at the village level, I will focus briefly on this theme in *Macbeth* and how the witches are either seen as village witches or as elite witches. I will then explore and relate this discussion to other plays particularly with the gender and class aspects of the witches' discourses (both village and elite) in *The Witch of Edmonton*. I hope to illustrate that *The Witch of Edmonton* represents behaviour other than the witch's power, as seen in *Macbeth* and something separate from the comical singing of the witches heard in *The Witch*. Rather, it depicts the notorious trials and executions of the witch-hunts in early modern England and how the witches in Middleton's *The Witch* aimed to satisfy their own lusts by sleeping with visitors, succubi and their own offspring. In Marlowe's *Doctor Faustus*, I will focus more on in the aspect of magic and how a magician attempts to reveal some hidden or secret powers of nature while this seeking power from nature itself is associated with bewitching and the world of witchcraft.

In Renaissance drama witches have features which are maternal rather than male. Because the mother figure readily intertwines with the witch figure this led to anxieties about the mother's role and her maternal power. In *Macbeth*, *Doctor Faustus* and *The Witch of Edmonton* and other plays, the problem of contemporary gender politics is clear, and as a result anyone who appears as a witch or magician usually must die by the end of the play. I will explore this theme and demonstrate why her/his life should be ended and the reasons behind this and also why the play requires anyone who has the role of witch and magician to play a rebellious role. Like many witchcraft papers, mine will be focused on the gender identity of the witch in early modern England and this contributes greatly to my understanding of what witchcraft and magic represented in that period.

This paper offers a historical background to writings on witchcraft by presenting three chapters: chapter one will present the nature of "the witch" and "magic" with examples of their different types in early modern England in general, illustrated by textual reference to some early Jacobean plays. It will also examine how the Jacobean dramatists used witch discourse in their plays to show the historical background of witches' trials and executions and the witch-hunts of that period. This study will consider the ideas of critics including Purkiss, Rosen, Oldridge, Gibson together with other critics and writers, involved in examining witchcraft and magic in early modern England.

The second chapter examines the different aspects of "village" and "elite" witch discourse with reference to each separate figure as depicted in the Jacobean dramas. By reviewing the ideas of some critics, I will focus on village witch and elite witch discourse and show how these present different beliefs and concepts. To take in all levels of witchcraft beliefs, popular and elite, one must understand to some extent the way of life of early England. This is because of the tensions between witchcraft and religion and the between magic and science and even with class conflicts: so there are echoes in literature of how witchcraft is viewed by its representation in the plays of that era and particularly Shakespeare. Taking a historical view it is clear that in the sixteenth and seventeenth centuries the Church of Rome was engaged in a life and death struggle with heresy. This led to those being suspected of heresy being insulted and doomed by a charge of witchcraft and use of magic because their accusers could find no better way of hurting them. However, the development of the physical sciences had a huge influence on people's mental attitude towards witchcraft and magic. The tension between magic and science had existed since the era of Newton and Descartes. Following that period, people's minds were increasingly familiar with the concept of natural law and the concept of natural death and natural disease. In his plays, Shakespeare is more concerned about witchcraft at the village level, which is rooted in the tensions among peasants and in particular focussed on women whom people believed brought death and sickness to their familiar and neighbours. This belief is the reverse of the positive role of the nurturing mothers and they were depicted as suckling their familiars at a third breast in order to highlight the contrast. Unlike the village witch, who believed in the theory of *maleficium*, the elite witch believed in other theories of witchcraft, such as having a pact with the Devil. It is more accurate to say that those who made the accusations against witches 'believed' in a variety of theories as we cannot be sure what the accused witches actually did. This study of village and elite witch discourses will consider the ideas of Purkiss, Holmes, Hall among other critics.

The third chapter will examine the gender representations of the male and female, in witchcraft beliefs and accusations, together with the anxieties apparent in Renaissance dramas by pooling a variety of critics' ideas with my own argument. In early England, there were doubts regarding the power that witches and magicians had to do harm or perform their tricks, and whether this hidden power was internally or externally acquired. This power is mysterious and harmful according to the popularly held belief, shared by women and men and which is at the heart of the concept of witchcraft which would manifest in certain women. Simple disputes could lead to accusations. Frequently, the witch and her victim would be neighbours and one woman might have been asked for something or some friendly service, which the neighbour had refused. This behaviour could lead to one being accused of being been a witch. Witchcraft at that time was used as an available excuse to attack women, that is why women were more vulnerable to accusations of witchcraft. Typically female pronouns have been used in relation to the idea of "witch" precisely because most of the people being accused of witchcraft were women rather than men.

The elderly women in early modern England were more prone to accusations of witchcraft rather than young females. Moreover, their aggressions tended to be indirect such as gossip, secret attacks and manipulating surrogates in contrast to males' direct aggressions focussed on physical violence. A physiological approach is also important in studying gender-relations in the era of witchcraft since the male biological and therefore perspective is different. This biological difference is linked to behaviour and the male direct aggressions in their acculturation. Historically, women tend not to use direct aggression, but tend to diminish the direct into the indirect through poisoning, battery and ritual magic while their foes sleep or are in an unconscious state. This is to counter the fact that physiologically men have muscular advantage and socioculturally have an image of specializing in social combat and can readily use complex weapons.

The idea that the male body is differently made and makes them think differently from the female, is an essentialist approach or in other words "men and women are essentially different". Fuss defines essentialism as "the idea that men and women, for example, are identified as such on the basis of trashistorical, eternal, immutable, "essence" has been unequivocally rejected by many anti-essentialist poststructuralist feminists concerned with resisting any attempts to naturalize "human nature"" (62). Some critics advocate the biological perspective of gender differences like the French feminist Helen Cixous, who believes men and women are essentially different. However, the American feminist Elaine Showalter believes that "simply to invoke anatomy risks a return to the crude essentialism, the phallic and ovarian theories of art, that oppressed woman in the past" (187). Showalter also further asserts that "Victorian physicians believed that women's physiological functions diverted about twenty percent of their creative energy from brain activity". And "Victorian anthropologists believed that the frontal lobes of the male brain were heavier and more developed than female lobes and thus that women were inferior in intelligence" (187). By considering the ideas of a variety of feminists, the approach of this dissertation involves gender interpretation in examining the feminine role of the victimized characters whose roles were viewed as being hysterical witches, magicians, and sorceresses in the Renaissance era. These roles also involve the witch, hysteric and sorceress ending up being destroyed. Furthermore, this paper asks if biological differences are related to indirect aggression of women by becoming witches and casting spells and the male advantage in the era of direct aggression or not. The study of witchcraft in relation to gender in this chapter will look at the works of Christina Larner, Marine Hester, Goodare, Simpson Holmes, Favret-Saada and various other works.

CHAPTER ONE

WITCHCRAFT AND MAGIC IN EARLY MODERN ENGLAND

---✦❖✦---

• Witches and Witchcraft

In this chapter the argument concentrates on the nature of the male and female "witch" and magic, looking at all available types such as witch or magician together with various beliefs in the area witchcraft. The idea of belief in witches might have originated from traditional folkloric fear or fantasies. Simpson points out that there are four components in the stereotypes of a witch which might or might not be present in any particular social group:

(1) A witch is someone who inflicts harm (*maleficium*) by magical means; this is a virtually universal and very ancient concept and has nothing learned about it.

(2) A witch is someone who gets magical power from the devil; obviously, this definition depends on a prior belief in a well developed religion which includes the concept of a personal devil (or a sinister deity such as Hecate), but it, too, is simple and widespread, and many historians would be content to call it part of popular culture.

(3) A witch is a member of a secret sect of Satan-worshippers who meet regularly and practise ritual murder, cannibalism and sexual orgies.

(4) A witch is not entirely human; he or she can fly by night, ride on strange animals or objects, and turn into an animal. (12)

Similarly, there is the idea that a witch works through the devil and harms by magical means as Gibson quotes from Gifford's sixteenth-century definition that a witch "is one that worketh by the Devill, or by some Devillish or Curious Art, either hurting or healing, revealing things secret, or foretelling things to come, which the Devill hath devised to entangle, and snare mens soules withal, unto damnation" (161). Gibson points out that the other sorts who are compassed to this circle are the Conjuror, the Enchaunter, the Sorcerer, the Deviner and "the Devill doth (no doubt) after divers sorts, divers forms deals in these: But no man is able to shew an essential difference in each of them from the rest" (161). However, a witch might be defined differently by other critics and writers, for example, Purkiss is paraphrasing Spretnak when she describes witches as:

> they bowed to no man, being the living remnant of the oldest culture of all-one in which men and women were equal sharers in a truly cooperative society before the death-dealing sexual, economic, and spiritual oppression of the Imperialist Phallic

Society took over and began to destroy nature and
human society. (9)

There is a cultural aberration that very few attempts have been
made to deal with the cases of witches and witchcraft. It would be
helpful a good deal to define witchcraft before pointing out the
types and nature of the witch and witchcraft. Rosenthal quotes
Weisman's definition of witchcraft according to Puritan clergy as
having "no mention either of ritual profanations such as the drinking
of murdered infant's [sic] blood or of any of the elaborate staging
devices so frequently found in Continental versions of the pact"
(600). Drawing on the ideas of the critics Kors and Peters, Oldridge
defines the concept of witchcraft in detail as:

> They sacrifice to demons, adore them, seek out and
> accept responses from them, do homage to them,
> and make them a written agreement or another
> kind of pact through which, by a single word, touch
> or sign, they may perform whatever evil deeds or
> sorcery they wish and be transported to or away
> from wherever they wish (...) In their sorcery they
> are not afraid to use the materials of baptism, the
> eucharist, and other sacraments. They make images
> of wax or other materials, which by their invocations
> they baptise or cause to be baptised. Sometimes they
> make a reversal of the holy cross, upon which our
> saviour hanged for us. Not honouring the mysteries,
> they sometimes inflict upon the representations and
> other signs of the cross various shameful things by
> execrable means. (4)

Witchcraft emerged in the later middle Ages in which era the concept of sorcery was transformed into witchcraft. Brooke draws on Weisman's points of view on the traditional definition of witchcraft as it was "rooted in an emerging dynamic of sponsorship and manipulation which developed between the magistrates and the "afflicted" witnesses (348). Witchcraft was rooted in sorcery and witches were not merely sorcerers but they also had interactions with demonic powers and added on some diabolical flourishes. And the churches were always afraid of the secret demonic agency of the witches with which they were supposed to have engaged in demonic invocation so as to bind themselves to demons. Witchcraft, Gaskill says, belongs to great shifts in the history of Western Europe: "state-building and legal centralization; the struggle to impose religious uniformity; population increase and economic competition; the reorganizations of social structure and relationships" (212). This explains that the idea of witchcraft sprang from human experience within specific cultural arenas instead of prosecuting dogma in one hand and community scapegoating on the other. The elite and the popular are two different dynamic components of witchcraft but not rival definitions of witchcraft. Gaskill also points out that witchcraft was "gendered, but not so as to facilitate male prosecution of women; women themselves were too bound up with the process of suspicion and accusation, and were stirred by the same fear and anger as men" (213).

The early modern period is considered as a turning point for the history of witchcraft in Europe. Baily argues that the word of "maleficium" literally in its origin means only "an evil or harmed deed, by implication one performed through magic" (961). Early modern people believed that witches worshiped demons and gave their souls to Satan so as to perform their magic by taking on his dark power. By drawing on the ideas of critic Nider, Baily stressed the difference between witches and necromancers thus: "in common usage they are called necromancers who, through a pact with demons [and] through faith in ceremonies, predict future events, or manifest certain hidden things by the revelation of demons, or who harm those around them by sorcery (*maleficiis*), and who often harmed themselves by demons" (983-984). One could say that both witches and sorcerers were found to be performing as the same evil tasks such as sexual orgies, infanticide and cannibalism once they had a pact with the demons.

There were different types of witches in early modern England but the most dangerous one was perceived as an old woman and the gender association with these types of witches has affected the concept of how they got their power and how they are motivated. Through their confessions in trials, some witches said, they acquired power through medicine which they purchased and not through inheritance. And some other witches might have got power when they became cattle owners and owned property. This kind of power that witches gained by medicine usually was used for their personal protection and sometimes for the good of the public. A good example of the anxiety provoked by belief in the superstitious powers attributed to witches in early modern England is provided in the witchcraft pamphlet W.W., *A true and just Recorde* (1582). This text from the British Library and Trinity College Cambridge, describes the events presented to a Brian Darcy, a Justice of the Peace, who questioned witches and later in 1585 became Sheriff of Essex (Gibson 77-78). The suspicion that she may have been employing witchcraft was brought against Ursley Kempe as a result of information provided by a lady named Grace Thurlowe. The allegation was that Grace's son, a child named Davy Thurlowe, had been behaving in a "strange and tormented" fashion. Ursley Kempe visits Grace to see how the child who was confined to bed is progressing. Apparently

Ursley goes in and out of the room three times, on each occasion holding Davy's hand and saying, "good child how are you." Later Davy sleeps better than previously, although it is noted "the palms of the child's hands are where the backs should be and the backs in the place of the palms." It later Transpires months earlier Grace and the nurse had disagreed after the birth of a "womanchild" and Ursley was forbidden to nurse this child which subsequently fell out of its cradle, broke its neck and died. Grace suspected Ursley of bringing her misfortune (presumably through witchcraft) as she had been very angry not to care for the child. Grace had apparently become lame and blamed this on Ursley. Ursley replied that she could "unwitche" but not "witche" and offers to show Grace how to be "unwitched", and we imagine this will cure Grace's lameness. Later, Ursley returns offering to do the "unwitching" for the sum of 12 pence. Grace agrees to this and five weeks later is cured. However, Grace then says she has no money and that she cannot pay Ursley with either cash or cheese. The two women fall out and Ursley says she will get even with Grace. This appears to happen as Grace becomes lame again permanently, and her child is "tormented". As will be explained subsequently, this example illustrates how in the sixteenth century the powers of good witches and bad witches were strongly believed to exist.

Simply put, there are two types of witches: good witches and bad witches. The good witches were supposed to be helpful and were seen as an advantage to the community in which they lived and did not work for a pittance. However, bad witches worked for ill-will and harmed their neighbours and they could easily change into a cat suddenly as a spiritual conduit of harm but this was not the case good witches. This is what accusers thought was possible. Both witches, good and bad, in the early modern period, worked by using different kinds of superstitious sources such as the spirit of holy men, e.g. Moses, Elias etc. Female and male magic used different instruments and a different library for their puzzles and tricks. However, as Rosen has highlighted that "the magician had many instruments and a library; the cunning man or woman might have a mirror or a perspective glass; the witch, good or bad, usually had nothing but a herbal remedy or two, several common-place spells, and an effective tongue for cursing or blessing" (ix.)

Sometimes shepherds known as "cunning men" were seen to be the cause of an animal's death which is different from the role attributed to that of the witch. Bever helps explain the meaning of the word "magic" as a means that women possessed to counter the fact that they had to take a subordinate social place because gender inequalities blocked legal possibilities for protection of their rights and interests. From Ahrendt-Schult 's studies on magic, Bever points out that the word for magical means is "Vergift" or "Venenum" in the language of fantasy. One kind of magical means that witches used was poison which shows that "witchcraft was not just some sort of idle fantasy or imaginary compensation, but an activity of the assertion of power. Poison could be used to kill an abusive husband, or in one specific case she discusses, a powerful male relative involved in a property dispute" (Bever, 959). The use of poison for magical purposes is one of the forms of sorcery and was a compound of herbal and remedial potions. People were also accused of malefic crimes of poisoning like with other witchcrafts: diabolism and ritual action. In trials, witches were accused of using poison to injure their neighbour's animals. Bever states, elite understood that they did not believe that the use of poisons involved a pact with the Devil or other forms of witchcrafts.

In Europe, it was mostly women who were held to be witches. Male witches were called warlocks or wizards, for example Merlin, the wizard of Arthurian legends. The Christian church as well as criminal courts often condemned single women and healers as witches, even if they were not known as the village wise women. Wise women were considered healers, and if you were sick, they would make up a medicine from herbs for the sick person to take, or make up a poultice to heal sores and aches and pains. However, the Wise Man has been characterized by Joseph Hall as "one who is not opposed to learning anything but who desires first to know his own strength and weakness, and to reduce his knowledge to practise rather than mere discourse" (qtd in McCullen 7). The Church and the criminal courts generally declared the wise women to be witches and condemned them as being under the influence of Satan, regardless of any good works they carried out.

Witchcraft might be seen as a violation of common sense and witch hunting as a means to maintain a clergy's power. Hall states that witchcraft belief in some communities was "endemic, not sporadic, and "real" in meeting certain social needs". Moreover, witchcraft was "functional, either because it affirmed village solidarity or because it relieved social strain" (253). This means that witchcraft belief was endemic and rooted in society's belief and did not vanished with the appearance of science; and also the fact that it was socially functional and considered real could be seen as social interaction among the villagers as a result of the conflicts between themselves. Hall points out that the actual number of witchcraft cases in England is much lower than contemporary Scotland and southern Germany: "in common law England torture was infrequent and witches were hanged, not burned as heretics" and because "for the most part English witches did not confess to participating in sexual orgies or the witch's sabbat"; they had not also signed any pacts with the devil (255).

Witchcraft as a power between the witch and Satan, in popular belief, was actually trivial and crude power. Magicians and witches always were condemned for their tricks and demonic acts. Moran argues that magic was condemned by the Orthodox clergy and Laity for its disregard of providential theology and its use of diabolical agency; and the practitioners of magic were attacked by Orthodox clergy and laity through mounting campaign against them (646). The accusation of women for witchcraft might be related to the idea that these alleged witches could not fulfil the men's opinion of how women should conduct themselves and women were responsible for their own spiritual salvation. The treatment of people with the suspected witches was not good: they were insulted and ostracised with their relatives; their husbands and sons might fired from their jobs with vandalizing their homes and wounded their pets. That is why the alleged witches led a very miserable life especially when they fell ill, they did not receive any help for anyone. This is because there was a belief that if somebody helped a witch in nursing, then the witch's power would pass into the one who had held her hand. This power was seen as a supernatural one as well as magic in the world of witchcraft.

• Magic

The use of supernatural power in magic can be good or evil and Schick quotes the definition of magic by Webster as "that art or body of arts which pretends, or is believed to produce effects by the assistance of supernatural beings or departed spirits, or by the mastery of the secret forces of nature" (1075). Schick suggests that one should use the word "magic" to describe those things that touch our emotions and imaginations, i.e. to describe what we cannot understand. Clark thinks that the "magician" was "someone who sought to ascend to acknowledge of these superior powers and then accentuate their normal workings by drawing them down artificially to produce wonderful effects" (217). The natural capacities that witches and magicians always in both genders are attempted to exceed is for demonic help. Having made pact with the devil or doing any deviant behaviour were accounted as witchcraft according the folk's perspective in early New England. Rosenthal argues that such a folk definitions rests on that magic is not originated from an acceptable theological form, the opinions of the elite ran counter popular belief in witchcraft who accepted witchcraft merely in their own theological terms (598).

In early modern England, witchcraft and magic became more disputable subjects in scientific and religious contexts. Clark explains that the contemporary term "magic" was descended from the *magia* of the ancient Persians (215). Agrippa defines Magick as it is

> "faculty of wonderful virtue, full of most high mysteries, containing the most profound contemplation of most secret things, together with the nature, power, quality, substance and vertues thereof, as also the knowledge of whole nature, and it doth instruct us concerning the differing, and agreement of things amongst themselves, whence it produceth its wonderful effects, by uniting the vertues of things through the application of them one to the other, and to their inferior sutable subjects, joyning and knitting them together thoroughly by the powers, and vertues of the bodies. This is the most perfect, and chief science, that sacred, and sublimer kind of phylosophy, and lastly the most absolute perfection of all most execellent philosophy". (qtd. in Clark 214)

Magic and necromancy can be considered as science and they have nothing to do with devils. However, if when devils achieved in both magic and necromancy is by the work of nature. This happens when the magician acquires knowledge from the evil angel or unclean spirit. The magician tries to reveal some hidden or secret things in nature. Hence, the works of nature or seeking for natural power is associated with bewitchment and the world of witchcraft.

Most of the writers are interested to know the unknown materials in Renaissance era and its impact on human lives. Magic and witchcraft were hot-button issues of that time. Many pamphlets and became the topic of many pamphlets as well as dramas. One of the Jacobean plays which centres on magic and superstitious power is Christopher Marlowe's *Doctor Faustus*, in early modern England. Marlowe is fond of the spirit of Renaissance and wants to reveal the hidden power under nature. As he is like anyone at that time, Faustus has a high ambition in having interest fro power. Ambivalence is appropriate, Gibson says, to the demonological subject: "the secret, forbidden world Marlowe created for the scholar Faustus is that of the Renaissance magus, a learned man who treads a dangerous line between satanic and divine, and who may or may not remain on the side of the angels" (172). Faustus shows himself to the reader as a Renaissance man against church, i.e. he is carless to the religious custom. He is curious to achieve facts about black magic and know limitless knowledge on black art. Faustus in his career tried to escape from the human condition through doing similar acts to Christ since he healed the sick and wanted to raise men from the dead and lived again. This leads him to sign a pact with the Devil with his own blood deliberately and by saying Christ's word on his lips.

Faustus's first attempt to conjurer, he started with the name of God, Tetragrammaton. He scarified to the Devil and then he wrote "Within this circle is Jehovah's name,/ Forward and backward anagrammatised" (A I. III. 80-10). Birringer states that Faustus as a heterodox doctor of divinity, he could eradiated all the "metaphysical distinction between body and soul, God and man, individual speech and cultural language" (338). He further states that Faustus touched upon the limits of the antitheological madness and writing himself over to the Devil in the crucial pact scene. Furthermore, when Faustus begins hallucinate, Birringer says, the words he sees and speaks are both his won and not own. Though the words he uttered, his destruction can be literary seen as a double actor, he does not merely speak from body but for his body:

> But what is this inscription on mine arm?
> Homo *fuge*! whither should I fly?
> If unto God He'll throw me down to hell,
> My senses are deceived, here's nothing writ,
> Oh yes, I see it plain! Even here is writ,
> Homo *fuge*! yet shall not Faustus fly. (ii.i.77-82)

Faustus pursuing knowledge is related to his own spiritual destiny and he destroys his live because of having not any knowledge of divine. Although form the beginning of the play he announced himself to be merely a "divine in show" (i.ii.3). He quoted some of his sayings from Bible especially when argues that "the reward of death is sin" (i.ii.38). McCullen argues that Faustus resurrects the logic he has just buried to discard both medicine and law with the inconsistency of a shallow mind. This is because "it cannot sustain life indefinitely or enable him to raise the dead; the other, because he considers it fit only for a mercenary drudge" (10). Faustus turned to magic in return to be offered a heavenly beauty incarnated and tried to convert his power of language into demonic lust and wanted to see human's aspiration through language. He was a kind of person who wanted to raise the dead to life again: "Wouldst thou make man to live eternally? / or, being dead, raise them to life again" (i.i.24-25). Faustus here wanted to compare himself with Christ and tried to see Christ's blood and ascend his soul to heaven: "My lips may issue from your smoky mouths,/ So that my soul may but ascend to heaven." (v.ii.94-95).

Faustus curious to revolt and does not care to religious costumes especially when Mephistopheles, the good angel, warns him. There is a scene of dismembering of Faustus's physical body when he is dead the good angel warning him, "if thou repent, devils shall [will] tear thee in pieces" (A i.iii.80) and also the analogous threat by Mephistopheles, "Revolt, or I'll in the piecemeal tear thy flesh" (A v.i.69). Furthermore, Faustus body had been pointed out by the second scholar's observation, "See, here are Faustus' limbs,/ All torn asunder by the hand of the death". The third scholar's pointed association to the devils: "The devils whom Faustus served have torn him thus/ For, 'twix the hours of twelve and one, methought / I heard him shriek and call aloud for help," (v.iii. 8-10). Mephistopheles and the other devils were able of linguistic cunning as by quoting the idea of critic William black burn, Benvington and Rasmussen argue that "not magic, but the magician, is on trial here'; the play 'is Marlowe's metaphor, not for the failure of language as an instrument of transformation, but for man's failure to understand it and use it wisely'" (39).

Dr. Faustus can be related to Marlowe's own blasphemous life and his death or, it might be commensurated with his artistic passion for the hero's failings and his destiny. As Dr. Faustus seems to be more personal and Marlowe's own blasphemous life. By Christian doctrine, a man needs merely repent and having a strong faith in order to be saved. Through his choice of necromancy, Faustus tells his audience that he damned himself in a conventional way which finally ended up with his self-destructiveness. He is much seen as a criminal one when he was under the sentence of death. His crime had inherited from his own humanity. The play shows that why Dr. Faustus must die rather than how to die as one can see it in the other Elizabethan plays. Ornstein stresses that Faustus was so arrogant, vain and guilty of cardinal sin of pride. This leads the reader that his "fall" is "neither a simple moral degradation nor a conventional seduction from conscience and belief" (1382). However, it is rather a moral education and discovery during which he was not degraded but humanized. Faustus as a learned man had trafficked with Satan like the common witches in order to obtain power and know secret things of life. It was thought that magician and witches both had casted spells for different money, luck and love and people were used to break these spells.

- **Spells against Witches:**

Both men and women are known to have done their magical practises, as men had professional skill at magical manipulation of disease and weather but women at black magic since they helped in ability to children giving birth. However, there were different means of breaking the spells according to different communities. Simpson points out what people had done to break the spells in different communities for example, in Britain,

> They boiled bottles of the victim's urine, but they also sprinkled it round the house as a productive charm; they used his or her faeces as a ointment (occasionally causing blood-poisoning), or smeared them all over the suspected witch's doorstep, in order to transfer the illness back to her. They

whipped their sick children in an attempt to break the spells on them. They would maim a dog or cat (ideally, one belonging to the witch), and drag it round the bewitched person or cow till it died. If these counterspells failed, the witchbuster would hold impressive cursing ceremonies, beating, burning or tearing clothes belonging to the sick person, or better still, something stolen from the witch's house. They might advice the victim to attack the witch and draw her blood. They took large fees for their work, and claimed the authority of God and the Bible for what they did; anyone who doubted their power was Christian. And whenever some old woman in the village feels ill, the local witchbuster claimed the credit. (10)

Sickness, misfortune and death were supposed to be caused by a spell. To remove the spell, the victims should use some "magic" items such as knotted rags, buttons threaded with hair, human or animal hair, and tangled feathers and these were all done by the witch- busters.

In order to annul the spell, in *The Witch of Edmonton*, there was attempt to scratch the face of Sawyer in order to remove the Maleficium by Ann Radcliffe. This was somehow a common belief that to injured a witch is annulled the spell. One of the most conventional dramatic elements that has been used in *The Witch of Edmonton* to show the reader the divine disapproval. The devil-dog was appeared as a result of Sawyer's anger for revenge: "Ho! Have I found thee cursing? Now thou art mine own" (ii.i.121). Corbin and Sedge argue that at that time Sawyer's response is ambiguous when Elizabeth Sawyer desires revenge and she is also fearful of giving up her soul. They further argue that it is important that Sawyer agrees to the pact merely "after the devil threatens to tear her into a thousand pieces. Thus it is a persecuted and isolated old women who is entrapped into witchcraft rather than an evil and malicious criminal who purposely seeks to acquire devilish power" (25). The dog sucked Sawyer's blood via her arm in aiding of thunder and lighting which can be considered as malevolent although the evils are carried out by the Dog once he killed the cattle of Old Banks by blighting the corn. The dog became Sawyer's familiar once she had a pact with him by selling her soul and body. However by the end of the play Sawyer cursed him as she realized he did not obey her: "Out Witch! Thy tryal is at hand: / Our prey being had, the Devil does laughing stand" (V.i.75-76). It indicates more the witch's anger, Sawyer's anger, when she is deserted by the Dog.

Mother Sawyer went to the gallows as she was convicted of witchcraft as well as Frank. Sawyer complains the community of Edmonton that she had been convicted because was "poor, deform'd, and ignorant,/ And like a bow buckled and bent together," (ii.i.3-4), and she had also only one eye: "Bless us, Cuddy, and let her curse her tother eye out. What dost now" (ii.i.89-90).She was sunned by her community as she was old, deformed, had one eye and some times as she stole some sticks to warm herself: "Gather a few rotten sticks to warm me" (ii.i.21). Unlike Mother Sawyer, one can find a comic witch figure who never been tortured and insulted by people in some Renaissance dramas.

- **Comic Witches:**

During the late of sixteenth century and early seventeenth century plays on witch were popular, in which the dramatists claimed to approach the social history of their community. Some of them were about witch trail and some others about witch-hunting. For example, Shakespeare's *Macbeth* is about the witch's power who can shape the man's destiny; *The Witch of Edmonton* is about notorious trails. However, Middleton's *The Witch* is not about witch's trail and execution in the witch-hunts. Instead, it shows the reader the comical singing of the witches who are never in any fear of being brought to trail and being tortured.

The Witch as Jacobean drama by Thomas Middelton has receives many scholarships on the relations between the supernatural scenes and the Hecate in association to *Macbeth*. The Witch is an ironic drama which is neither comedy and nor tragedy or it can be called a middle mood play and dealing more with the dilemmas of ordinary people. Unlike Shakespeare's witches, Middleton used the witches for impotency and preventing of having sex during the consummating of the characters. For example, by having the aid of the witches, Sebastian could prevent Isabella from consummating her marriage to Antonio. The witches could render Antonio's impotency. Schoenbaum argues that Middleton's witches are less interested in shaping men's destinies than in satisfying their own lusts by sleeping with "visitors or succubi or their own offspring; their escapades reflect the persistent concern with sexuality that is to lead the dramatist, in his mature tragedies, into psychological explorations unattempted by his contemporaries" (9). In *The Witch*, the witches were not merely themselves but they had also Hecate to guide them and meeting with them.

- **Hecate in both Macbeth and The Witch:**

The supernatural figures, in *The witch*, are Hecate and her cohorts who are not a goddess but Hecate does fly and can run witch's meeting, coven, and cook dead infants, and all the other things that witches were believed to do such as: casting spell, having familiars and some more other activities. Schafer hints of stage history of the witch scenes in *The Witch*, and considers them as a strongest aspect of the play. She argues that the witch scenes are entertaining and "visually impressive, and there is a powerful dramatic tension produced by the juxtaposition of the wild, fantastic and funny witch scenes with the moody, troubled and murderous court scenes" (xxvi). She further states that the witch scenes tend to upstage the court scenes and mock them.

It is said that *Macbeth* and *The Witch* have some shared scenes especially in the witch scenes. Purkiss illustrates that like the witches in Macbeth, "Hecate's appearances are staged as a queasy mixture of decontexualised village-stories muddled with the more striking and spectacular features of continental lore" (218). In *Macbeth* the witches are called haggish since Banquo called them "withered" and "wild" in their attire: "So withered, and so wild in their attire, / That look not like th' in habitants o' th' earth/ And yet are on't?- live you, or are you aught/ That man many question? You seem to understand me" (i.iii.40-44). He also states that their masculine shapes confused him to know who the are: "By each at once her choppy finger lying/ Upon her skinny lips. You should be women, / And yet your beard forbid me to interpret / That you are so" (i.iii.44-48). Similarly, in *The Witch*, Sebastian also states that the appearance of Hecate is horrific and fearful and then he calls her "hag": "Whate'er thou art, I have no spare time to fear thee" (i.ii.119). Hecate is called "hag" when Sebastian says: "That I may never need this hag again" (i.ii.179). Hecate, in another scene with Firestone, is called "foul": "I am sure they'll be a company of foul sluts there tonight" (iii. iii.16-17). The problem here is that witch figure is called hag and has a bad reputation in the plays above. In terms of gender and feminist approaches, staging witch as hag can be analysed and disputed through gender stereotype. The reader is not impressed and interested by stereotype hags. The witch scenes in *The Witch* condemn the corrupt society of early modern England instead of centering on individuals.

The Witch is seen by so many critics as a recapitulation of a story from elsewhere, Shakespeare' *Macbeth*, especially in the dance and singing scenes of the witches. Purkiss argues that the story of France Howard has been found in *The Witch* in the scene that the cunning woman, Anne Turner, the woman whom Howard allegedly consulted about keeping her husband impotent, in relation to Middleton's Hecate. Purkiss stresses that Hecate is less a witch than the embodiment of witchcraft, witchcraft mad into action or made of capable of action (216-217). What distinguish Anne Turner from Hecate is in its ending: Hecate was survived and neither punished to death nor repentance and retribution. However, Anne Turner underwent to repentant and reintegrated into the community and punished to death. Hecate like Shakespeare's witches exists merely in the midnight in the coven and her own abode. Purkiss considers Hecate not a "real" person, but a *witch*. Hecate, Purkiss argues, did not have place in "the larger society or familial structures which she serves and disrupts; even though she has a son/lover, this does not amount to social integration, but is yet another signifier of her apartness, her disorder" (219).

One of the supernatural powers used in *Macbeth* is the witches mighty goddess of destiny: Hecate. The witches are named as "the Weird Sisters" who are "creatures of an elder world", Tolman notes, and they can not be questioned. During the period when *Macbeth* was written, witches were considered a reality and Tolman argues that "the world of witchcraft was dark and mysterious, but it was real" (208). He also points out that when *Macbeth* appeared, "the entire English people, king and subjects, believed in the reality of witchcraft" (211).

In contrast to Tolman, Bradley points out that the witches in *Macbeth* "are not goddesses, or fates, or in any way whatsoever, supernatural beings. They are old women, poor and ragged, skinny and hideous, full of vulgar spite..." (298-299). He then argues that Macbeth was tempted solely by himself since he speaks of their supernatural soliciting but actually they did not solicit this. They merely foreshadowed his future in announcing the three titles for him. In contrast, Purkiss argues that the witches in *Macbeth* are in fact witches, rather than simply odd old women. The language of their speech "is marked off from that of the other characters in a manner which insists on their iconic status and also on their difference from the human". In addition, she also points out that witches are not "ordinary women who have sinned, but a special class of being, like monsters or mermaids" (210). Contrastingly, drawing on the idea of the critic Curry, Muir argues that the Weird Sisters are not in fact witches, but demons or devils in their form: "whether one consider them as human witches in league with the power of darkness, or as actual demons in the form of witches, or as merely inanimate symbols, the power which they wield or represent or symbolizes is ultimately demonic" (liv).

Nosworthy also concentrates on both Hecate's role and appearance in *Macbeth* and *The Witch*. He argues that Hecate appears as a very different creature in Middleton's *The Witch*: "she is coarse, brusque, and colloquial, speaking mainly in blank verse, occasionally in irregular rhyming verse, and never in octosyllabic couplets", however, Hecate's *Macbeth* "employs just those couplets for polished speeches of distinctly Senecan flavour" (138). Gibson believes that 120-yeard-old Middleton's Hecate witch was created probably between 1613 and 1915. She also argues that it obviously origins both in European demonologies such as the *Malleus Maleficarum* and the *Malleus* in Scot's English scepticism. Hecate's witches are described by Gibson as "lecherous, murderous and perverse in the traditional demonological way, but they are also funny, vulnerable and uncomfortably necessary to the maintenance of state power and social position by hose who resort to them" (97).

- **Other Witch Figures:**

There numerous terms in English in reference to the world of superstition such as: witch, sorcerer, wizard, magician, conjuror, war-lock and some times they are followed an adjective such as: good/ bad witch, cunning man/woman, black/white witch, and wise man/woman. Simpson explains that the cunning man/woman, wise man/women, white witch and good witch are too broad traditional terms which are used as a specialist traditional magic for other helpful purposes such as healing or detecting thieves. However, the others such as conjuror, sorcerer and wizard are ambiguous and often applied to harmful magicians (5). The "good" witches or white witches are healers and midwives who were prosecuted and were suspected by men. It is thought that these women, "healers" derived their healing powers to heal sick people from the alleged sources such as the dead or fairies.

Male witches or warlocks were rarer, but that may have been at times because women were the easy targets for the Churches rage against such practices. Anderson and Gordon state the belief in the innate inferiority of women and it seems to have done little to transform prevailing attitudes toward women in sixteenth and seventeenth centuries. As Catholic and Protestant societies were alike towards women's status and improving it markedly. They argue that scapegoating of women as witches was possible and "became effective only because there still existed in late medieval and post-Reformation Europe a powerful framework of denigrating beliefs relating women which those who constructed the stereotype witch and initiated the moral panic could draw in a credible way" (174). This is because women's nature, Anderson and Gordon say, were felt to be more corruptible than men but that means that the fact that most witches were women was not accident. In contrast to this, Kieckhefer believes that "it was precisely *because* of the feminine weakness they possessed that the Devil sought out women to be his agents and helpers, so that any campaign against witches implicitly entailed elements which were directed against women" (qtd. in Anderson and Gordon 174).

In other countries, especially North America, the women who carried out such practices appear to be more of a minority, as the witch doctor, or shaman was usually male and often had as much power within the tribes as the chief himself. Walker argues that witches and shamans "embody this dualism in the behavioural sense that both manipulate spiritual powers in their ritual activities. Shamans heal and witches destroy but both employ powers that often have the same supernatural source, and therefore shamans is always under the suspicion of witchcraft, and the witch may if reformed act as a shaman" (265). In the African continent and in Australia, there were, and are still, female and male witches and witchdoctors who carry out the shamanistic traditions of their various tribes. These traditional practices have been carried on for generations and their methods continued by word of mouth and by initiation and demonstration from the older shaman to the initiate. Howitt states that the term "Doctor" or "Blackfellow Doctor" is always used in Australia for those men in a native tribe who profess to have supernatural powers" (24). He also explains that this term cannot be considered correct if by the word "Doctor" one means that someone who use some means of curing disease. This is because, Howitt says, "the powers these men claim are not solely those of healing, nor even those of causing disease, but also such as may be generally spoken of as magical. Thus the doctors are in this sense magicians and wizards" (24).

In Africa witchcraft rests on the social relations and contexts of interaction. Lyons in his enthnoarchaeological study of witchcraft in Africa argues that "in African societies witchcraft perceived as a personal act of one individual drawing upon preternatural powers to harm another. This behaviour is purposive: it is a strategy used within particular sets of social relations and contexts of interaction" (344-345). Most of the African accusations of witchcraft are between peers, kin and co-wives. In Europe, especially in England, the power of the Church over the population has declined over the past thirty to forty years. This has led to a relaxation of the standard of how to live within certain guidelines in order to live a good and civilised life. However, the loss of general spirituality has left a vacuum for beliefs. Together with a more relaxed attitude to life and how you live it in general, the 'Old Ways' as they were called, are now coming much more into prominence as people are more prepared to speak about their spiritual experiences which may have had no connection with the Church at all.

Consequently, the appreciation of natural earth energies, for example ley lines, is now quite openly discussed, and people speaking of such things are not always regarded as crazy. Moreover, the old Wicca traditions are now being quite openly celebrated, for example Beltane is the celebration of summer. Wicca is the practice of worshipping the natural earth energies and the energies or spirits which live within all living things, e.g. trees, flowers, animals, as well as people. Hutton declares that Wicca had been essentially been created by a man, retired colonial official named Gerald Gardner.

Hutton in his article on the difference and distance of Wicca to ancient paganism has suggested that "Wicca was distinctive in its duotheism, its veneration of a single goddess and god; in its regular summoning and invocation of those deities into the bodies of worshippers, who would then represent them to the other initiates present; and its common use of ritual nudity" (104-105). Druids are also quite openly practising and speaking the old Celtic languages and they were the high priests of very old days.

In conclusion of this chapter one can say that there were different representations of witches in early modern England. Most of them were representing the real historical witches and some might not. Through the definitions of the critics for "Witch", "magic" and witchcraft, It has been clear that the "good" witches or white witches are healers and midwives who were prosecuted and were suspected by men. It is thought that these women, "healers" derived their healing powers to heal sick people from the alleged sources such as the dead or fairies. "Bad" witches and sorcerers were found as they were doing the evil task such as sexual orgies, infanticide and cannibalism once they had a pact with the demons. And most of the women were not witches but their societies made them to choose this identity. These all figures were reflected on Renaissance writers and dramatists to write their pamphlets and their dramas on witchcraft in that era. One of the example, that the paper brought in was *The Witch of Edmonton* in which the heroic character was originally was not a witch but the villagers made her a witch.

In another section, the paper has focused on magic and its reflection on dramas, in particular Marlowe's *Doctor Faustus*. Magicians and witches always were condemned for their tricks and demonic acts by the churches and the criminal courts. Doctor Faustus tried to reveal some hidden or secret things in nature which was associated with bewitchment and the world of witchcraft. Doctor Faustus singed a pact with the devil to commit a sin of demoniality and without repenting. In *Doctor Faustus* like the other Elizabethan plays, Dr. Faustus as a magician hero played a role that he must die rather than how to die. Mother Sawyer was also another witch victims went to the gallows as she was convicted of witchcraft as well as Frank. In opposite to *The Witch of Edmonton*, Middleton's *The Witch* shows the reader the comical singing of the witches who are never in any fear of being brought to trail and being torture. During the period when *Macbeth* was written, witches were considered a reality. So, Hecate scenes in both *Macbeth* and *The Witch* has been focused on which was used as a superstitious dramatic device to show that witches in the shape of Hecate. However, historically Hecate witch not is not close to the real historical witches by which Hecate in the dramas was survived and never repented and punished to death which might not meet with the historical case of Hecate witch.

CHAPTER TWO

VILLAGE WITCH AND ELITE WITCH

In order to understand early modern England's life, one should look at all the levels of witchcraft beliefs, popular and elite, because of having had many religious tensions, tensions between magic and science with class conflicts Witchcraft has echoed in literature by representing it in the plays of that era and especially Shakespeare's plays. Holmes argues the matter of witchcraft in relations to gender roles and he thinks that most of the accusations conformed can be considered as a product of a social process. For example,

> Nicholas Starkey's children, aged nine and ten, delighted in "filthie and unsavoury speeches"; they scoffed at Scripture as "bible bable, bible bable"; the boy bit his mother and called her "whore"; Margaret Byrom, a poor kinswoman who lived on the Starkey family's charity, "nick-named and taunted" her

benefactors (…) in which key roles were played by adults and males. The possessed adolescents were the tools of the divines; their dramatic performances reinforced the witchcraft-as-diabolic-covenant theology, with its ancillary emphasis upon the frailty of the "weaker sexe" in the face of satanic temptation. (65)

Men also with women became a target of accusation of witchcraft. So gender plays a vital role in witchcraft allegations. The function roles of men and women were discussed and people in western Europe were working hard to impose the new forms of Christian patriarchy society. Most of the prosecuted men were associated with the female witches when they went to the stake and some of them were the witch's brother, son or husband. Women were seen by people as a tool of demons and devils as they were weak in devil's temptation.

Witches had always a lower position and not been considered as virtue people in the society. Atkinson argues that, in *The Witch of Edmonton*, the witch, Mother Sawyer and Frank Thorney, "are hardly to be though to as especially virtuous people, but neither are they intentionally wicked; in fact they show little consciousness of the difference between right and wrong" (420). Sawyer can be seen as malevolent since she revenged upon Old Banks but this was happened as her natural aggravation but not as her conscious evilness. If one look at the social hierarchy of the play, Sir Arthur Clarington has the top position but the middle, country men and peasants occupied and the lower position is given to the witch, Elizabeth Sawyer, whom had been feared and abused by her neighbours.

Similar to *The Witch of Edmonton*, both plays *The Witch* and *Macbeth* begins with the high social position as royal gentleman and then country men and the witches had lower position. In his plays, Shakespeare more concerned about village level which is rooted from the tensions among the women of peasants whom people believed that they bring back death and sickness to their neighbours. This kind of belief is reversed the positive role of nurturing mothers, because they were suckling the familiars at a third breast. Hale states that "Gentry-level" or elite discourses sees witches "as subordinate to Satan, treasonably transferring political and religious allegiance to an alternate male figure" (662). Hale also points out that the general direction of elite discourse was to differentiate "the Protestant form the Catholic practice, part of a more general, national interest in social order and patriarchal hierarchy" (662). The itch-prosecution in Early Modern England is very complex because it involves in many cultural groups. Early modern male elites thought that women were more vulnerable to the Devil's blandishments however its common people, both women and men, thought that women were expected to utilize their power against them. Favret-Saada argues that rural witches believed in the theory of maleficium and practised witchcraft well before the sixteenth century. The elite witches believed the other theories such as satanic pact with Devil and black masses but having prosecuted them must necessarily have been added to the rural one (574). Because of having brought complaints from the local people and peasants to the authority, witch trial and witch prosecution took place. Traditional belief in malevolent witches was a familiar one among the peasants in contrast to the diabolical witches. The witch trails revealed that how the witches did their witchcraft and necromancy.

The witch believes and accusations reflected through exercising and precipitating of the power. Men also side by side women exercised their magical power and victims in the witch trails. There are different kinds of witch accusations: some of the old women were accused by their better-off neighbours and some of them in reverse: the well-to-do alleged witches were accused by their poorer popular people while there were other, the accused and the accusers, were economically roughly in the same station. However, most of the witch accusations sprang from the personal conflicts of the villagers through gossiping, scolding and curses while they were peaceful and friendlier than the elite people. Drawing on the idea of critic Briggs, Bever argues that those women were known as "sorceresses were equally feared for their readiness to use their magical powers as weapons in conflicts with their neighbours" (959).

The witch trials showed women in the history of witchcraft and women used the source of power through witchcraft more than the men in early modern England. And this power was stemmed from popular belief and elite beliefs. First time the popular people believed witchcraft but then the state and church shared witchcraft believes and could suppress the popular culture slowly in the cities. The early modern trials were taken place for discrediting magical beliefs when the witches were taken to their extreme. The witch trails can be seen as a form of acculturation that elite culture wanted to expand its dominance on popular culture. The trial prosecutions had influence on women's behaviours and their attitude toward witchcraft. This change in their behaviour was taking pace by considering male's violence toward women in the late of seventeenth century and women violence was also about to waning once the public authority were concerned about them. The prosecutions were not putting to death but instead of that they were tortured, jailed, banished and some of them were under the eyes of their neighbours for the rest of their lives.

According to Murray's view on witches, female and male, "was a hideous spiteful old hag is entirely erroneous" by the modern popular believe. He also affirms that male witches were as much as females whereas they participated natural magic in the affairs of the sate and sat on the Council of the King. They were sometimes the rulers of the realm once they wielded the power. However, in the villages they were "the advisers for all illness of mind and body" (...) the male witch often wore "a kind of uniform to distinguish him from the folk" and the female witch "was decked with black lambskin and white catskin, with polished with metal and shining stones" (227). Witches were not merely suspected by their neighbours but some of them were named by the arrested witches under torture. Women's witchcraft was not like that of men since their witchcraft was more linked to their sexual identity. For example, in one kind of process of witch-hunting in Scotland, some of the witches pricked their body with pin until a spot was found. Goodare argues that the pricker of males was mostly found in their back, shoulder and thigh but women's was in their "privy parts" after they confessed to it (302). So this type of witch's mark seems to be an idea of demonology in elite demonology context as intellectual belief since they thought that the Devil nipped on witch's body when their demonic pact was made between them.

As English village wives and doctors searched for the witch marks of the accused witches. By looking at Goodcole's work, Purkiss argues that the same situation happened to Elizabeth Sawyer in *The Witch of Edmonton* village who was searched by the "specially appointed jury of matrons, and the searchers apparently found a thing like a teat, the bigness of the little finger the length of half a finger, which was branched at the top like a teat, and seemed as though one had sucked it" (241). The relationship between Elizabeth sawyer and her familiar appeared through the sucking of her blood and then forming a teat in her body as a witch's mark: "I am dried up/ With cursing and with madness, and have yet/ No blood to moisten these sweet lips of thine" (iv.i.153-6). The alleged witches were supposed to use their familiar's body for deceit. Purkiss points out that the shifting colour of the dog, in *The Witch of Edmonton*, pointing to its unreliability and deceptiveness, signifying to the instability of identity which is more "emphasized by his curiously lengthy explanation of how he comes by bodies to use" (246). The dog's body is seen to be used for deceit and ill-will since he equated himself to the devil theatrically: "I'll shug in, and get a noble countenance;/ Serve some Briarean footcloth-strider/That has an hundred hands to catch at bribes,/ But not a finger's nail of charity" (v.i.183-6).

The writers, in *The Witch of Edmonton*, have focused on Elizabeth Sawyer's evil power to change the borderlines between human, the witch, and animal, her suckling familiar. She was more closed to animals, Purkiss argues, and the witch's punishment of her enemies involves forcing them to cross the line between animal and human, "I have heard old Beldams/ Talk of Familiars in the shape of Mice,/ Rats, Ferrets, Weasels, and I wot not what,/That have appeared, and sucked, some say, their blood" (ii.i.102-5). And she called her enemies sucking animals when she says "this black cur/That barks and bites, and sucks the very blood/ of me and of my credit" (ii.i.111-113). Purkiss stresses on Sawyers' body that is presented in the play as more prone to "leak" words than blood: "she offers the "teat" to her familiar, but also apologises fro being dry through cursing" (iv.i.145-7). Purkiss hints at Sawyer's cursing role as a character dramatically, socially and medically:

She is a choleric, overflowing with the hot blood of the dog das, blood that is dried up by her furies. She is the stage-type of the elderly shrew, whose humorous makes her cursed. Dramatically, the play substitutes the sound of cursing for the sight or site of the witchmark, a bodily truth of the body as speech, cursing is an expression of the hot blood which would otherwise leak out or be fed to the dog. The fact that the dog-demon arrives as Sawyer is cursing is usually read socially: cursing is a transgression of gender roles. But it can also be read medically: cursing is a sign of hot red blood overflowing, a sign to which a familiar is naturally attracted (242).

Dekker wants to portray the poor condition of witch in seventeenth century and show they were living in sordid poverty in opposite to the wealth of the sorcerer through the role of Sawyer. Elizabeth Sawyer was showed as the power of an old woman in the village of Edmonton who did a real harm and she acted as a village witch not elite.

The Renaissance plays mostly focused on witches and witchcraft belief and separated themselves from the popular belief, theatrically. In *The Witch of Edmonton*, the dramatists stressed the popular belief of witchcraft by casting three dancers in the morris dancing and equated dancing with witchcraft:

Young Banks. (…) Have we e'er a witch in the morris?
First Dancer. No, no; no woman's part but Maid Marian and the hobby-horse.
Young Banks. I'll have a witch. I love a witch.

> First Dancer. 'faith, witches themselves are so common now-a-days that the counterfeit will not be regarded. They say we have three or four in Edmonton besides Mother Sawyer.
> Second dancer. I would she would dance her part with us. (iii.i.7-15).

Here the witch is displayed as a role and but the dancers suggested that the real witch should act as a one. This is made clear in the play through Elizabeth Sawyer, her role was increasingly casted as a witch. She was as a witch was a frightening female form through her tongue and her body, on the other hand. "to creep under an old witch's coats and suck like a great puppy! Fie upon't! I have heard beastly things of you, Tom" (v.i.173-174). This further shows Young Bank's fear to the dog's willingness to suck Sawyer's blood like a great puppy. This also emphasised further on the gender issue that female body had been used in the context of anxieties in lactating body of the woman as a witch. The stage showed its audience how was the figure of witch and witch hunting in the seventeenth century.

However, there is another Jacobean play that trace elite magic and witchcraft contexts which is Marlowe's *Doctor Faustus*. Faustus gets started with black magic as a blasphemous choice of his art at the beginning of the play but then his role was ended up with despair and dread moments by the end of the play. As Ornstein points out that from the beginning, mean sensual appetites intermingle with Faustus' Promethean aspirations and he was too glutted with self-conceit to see that his mastery over Mephistophilis. This was mere appearance and that he defied heavenly law only to accept the bondage of hell. Ornstein also argues that hungering for immortality, Faustus "traded his hope of salvation for twenty-four years of pleasure and profit, but even the terms of this ridiculous bargain are not honour, because he never attained the powers or the knowledge which magic promised" (1380).

In another hand, popular magic can be appeared in Faustus magic since in popular belief witches used kiss as a means of doing their magic and wickedness toward others. In *Doctor Faustus*, Helen has given an ambiguous female figure in the play and Faustus thinks of her as another succubus when Mephistopheles offered him. This demonic offer can be seen as a kind of temptation to Faustus as he says:

> Sweet Helen, make me immortal with a kiss:
> Her lips sucks forth my soul. See where it flies!
> Come, Helen, come, give me my soul again. (A V.i.92-4).

Kiss in the witch context might relate to the belief that witches pass on their familiar to somebody else through a kiss before they pass away. Tate stresses on this scene of kiss and he believes that kiss for Faustus, enabling the knowledge and acts as a surrender of "the beholding of heavenly beauty" which is the knowledge of God" (267). It is believed that Faustus was lost once he kissed Helen and was seen as a succubus. Faustus considers Helen as "spirit" and the spirit to him is devil when he says: "Her lips sucks forth my soul. See where it flies". Faustus's sin of demoniality is that having bodily intercourse with demons and bartering his soul into the demonic power, evil power. The kiss here is the bodily intercourse with Helen, "spirits", and it is the ultimate signal of sin of demoniality. Keissling's view on Faustus's sin of demoniality is that that is a kind of inverted pride that prompts Faustus "to regard his sin as worse than that of Satan himself. He also reveals that his sin had more to do with books than sheer sensuality", "would I had never seen Wittenberg, never read book" (xix.41-45) (211).

Faustus's tragic story is stemmed from the inadequacy of his knowledge once he was lured to dump himself to the companionship of devils or i.e. having wanted proper information was the cause to his rebellion and then his despair. Doctor Faustus singed a pact with the devil to commit a sin of demoniality and without repenting. Cox argues that Doctor Faustus committed all six of the sins which were traditionally characterized as to be sins against the Holy Ghost: "Faustus is guilty not only of presumption and despair, sins which Dame Helen correctly identified as two of the sins against the Holy Ghost, but also of impenitence, obstinacy, resistance to the known truth, and envy of a brother's spiritual good" (120). In committing sin against the Holy Ghost, it had two significant effects on Faustus which makes his domination ambiguous and on the other hand, it helps to clarify the sense in which Faustus's fall is tragic (122). He more relied on the devil rather than God since the devil was more real to him rather than God. Hunter's view on Marlowe's Dr. Faustus, he believes that after Faustus has signed away his soul "the first fruits of his new "power ... honour ... omnipotence" appear in the knowledge of astronomy that he seeks". Astronomy is a heavenly art, Hunter states, "no doubt – it appears early in the encyclopaedias – but it is one that is not obviously dependent on divinity" (84).

Cox argues that Faustus has only two choices to repent or to persevere when he said "I do repent, and yet I doe despair". These two choices "both heightens the suspense and suggests that sin by custom has nearly grown into nature" (131). Therefore, having not feared in God's justice led him to commit his first sin against the Holy Ghost. Faustus's despair of God's mercy is shown in a scene that he was hesitate in singing the bond with Lucifer and chose the decision un-thoughtfully:

> Now, Faustus, must
> Thou needs be damn'd, and canst thou not be sav'd.
> What boots it, then, to think on God or heaven? Away
> with such vain fancies, and despair; Despair in God,
> and trust in Belzebub. (n, i, 1-5)

When the good angel tried to turn Faustus away from the art of magic, "Sweet Faustus, leave that execrable art./ Faustus. Contrition, prayer, repentance-what of them?" and argued him that contrition, prayer and repentance as the "means to bring thee unto heaven" (ii.i.13—16). However, he was distracted by the evil angel when he reminded Faustus honour and wealth. Therefore, Faustus casted his lot with evil: "When Mephistopheles shall stand by me,/ What god can hurt thee, Faustus? Thou art safe;/ Cast no more doubt. Come, Mephistopheles,/ And Bring glad tidings from great Lucifer./ Is't not midnight? Come, Mephistopheles!" (ii.i.24-28). Faustus' fall came from his own willpower acting deliberately in the process of signing his soul. McCullen states that in spite of Faustus's folly and evil evident, the effect of his role is different and his spiritual welfare remains in doubt till the last scene of the play. He also stresses that it was not "his pact with Lucifer that constitutes his unpardonable sin, and, though he has already thought f despair, there is nothing inescapable about the hold it as yet exerts upon him" (13). Faustus's pursuit of magic, "which carries him on diverting flights throughout the world, and the foolish tricks he plays on others also provide little more satisfaction than a momentary escape from his spiritual problem. In both he is like the slothful condemned" (14). Faustus has been portrayed in the play as a transformation character from a sinful man into a hardened sinner after having committed six sins against the holy ghost. McCullen states that the characteristic of Faustus's study is a "habit of culling form reading whatever his readings details strike his fancy. His inward conflict is the result of this erroneous approach to learning, and his boasted wisdom is nothing more than his own delusion" (11). Faustus arrogantly proclaims and praises the virtue of magic: "Now Faustus, thou art conjuror laureate,/ That canst command great Mephistophilis" (i.iii.34-35).

Most of the Renaissance plays such as Shakespeare's *Macbeth*, *The Witch of Edmonton* and *The Witch* are all merely drawn from popular and folklore superstition but Marlowe's *Doctor Faustus* is more the speculation of philosophy. By drawing on the idea of critic Masinton, Eccles quotes that Marlowe's picture of Faustus is "probably autobiographical" and Faustus is both "the arch-protestant" and the first tragic man"; and "his damnation is the existential plight of the radical humanist", so that he represents "the failure of Renaissance man". He further interprets Doctor Faustus not merely as a tragedy but a "spiritual biography of Western man in Renaissance and modern periods" (403-404).

One can find a comparable condition between Elizabeth Sawyer's misapprehensions of her relationships with the Dog with the situation of *Doctor Faustus*. Faustus and Sawyer, each of whom has to consider repentance after a pact, but which seems to be an element shared by both popular and elite discourses of witchcraft. Atkinson points out that repentance for Sawyer might still be possible because "Faustus, although he has similarly sealed with his blood a pact with the Devil, is urged until the very last moment to repent and be saved" (432). He further finds that there is some doubt in Sawyer's ultimate fate: "she goes to her execution there is non of the forgiveness and reconciliation that accompany Frank and nobody expresses the conviction that she will achieve salvation" (462). Finally, Mother Sawyer left the stage with difficulty and a new measurement of goodness in her repentance:

These Dogs will mad me: I was well resolv'd
To die in my repentance; though 'tis true,
I would live longer if I might: yet since
I cannot, pray torment me not; my conscience
Is setled as it shall be: all take heed
How they believe the Devil, at last hee'l cheat you.
Have I scarce breath enough to say my Prayers?
And would you force me to spend that in bawling?
Bear witness, I repent all former evil;
There is no damned Conjurer like the Devil. (V.iii.41-51)

Faustus as a magician gained power by selling his blood to the Devil but in return, he had to pay the penalty his bargain in a horrible death by the end of the play. Herrington is in the believe that Faustus has Marlowe's hunger, hunger for power and experience. Since the protagonist takes the most tremendous of all steps: "he contracts his immortal soul to the Devil for the delights of knowledge, sensual indulgence, and power; persists, withal, in his contract, though frequently wavering and repentant; and at length, when the time is out, delivers his soul in horrible agony to the fiend" (461).

The use of magic as a dramatic device in *Doctor Faustus* is different from that of Thomas Middleton's. Middleton in *The Witch* appears to his reader as an ironist and didactic dramatis of which his main theme is that the audience can learn through experience. However, this experience can merely be a corrupt. Middleton by the use of the witches wants to show his reader that he uses magic, as an important dramatic device, in casting spell which works like a charm. The witches of Middleton, Gibson states, "are an organized a Satanic cult, with references to their witches' "master" and to their taking of oaths, but despite a hodge-podge of grotesque detail, they seem really rather harmless" (97-98). Middleton used this idea to satirize

Catholic European belief in witches and magic when the cunning women casted spell for women in order to make their husband impotent. And the women could a divorce and marry their lovers. So, witchcraft in *The Witch* is used as a subject matter for satire on human wickedness.

Hall stresses on the distinction between popular belief and learned belief of witchcraft of which "according to conventional wisdom belief in maleficium was "popular" and in diabolism, or the idea of the devil's compact, "learned"" (276). Witchcraft far back into popular belief which was based on specific harms attributes to the woman's malice power instead of having the dangers of the Devil with the nature for the evil. The witches in *Macbeth* are in fact a reflective figure of the English village witch. Since the characteristic of Lady Macbeth is considered as witch by some critics, could be analyzed in village witch discourse. *Macbeth*, the play was ambivalent since the restoration of patrilineal role of Malcolm was an implicit order. And the idea of maternal malevolence was displayed by the aristocratic witch, Lady Macbeth and the lower-class witches, the three sisters. The features of Lady Macbeth's maternal figure can be seen in village witch discourse rather than elite ones. She tries to acquire a magic power, as a village witch, through her maternal power to harm others, and she misdirects her malevolent maternal power and fill it in with demonic thought instead. She asks the spirit to remove her biological femininity, not merely the psychological, but to take her means of procreation and any sensitive feelings associated with her femininity by saying "Come, you spirits/ That tend on mortal thoughts, unsex me, here" (1.v.38-39). During Shakespearean time, tales of village witchcraft became more evident and the village witch became a sign for events in the public sphere. Shakespeare's first witch refers to sailing in a sieve which

Rosen points out that sailing in a sieve seem to originate from folktales which deal with an 'impossible task':

> *First Witch,* Where has thou been, sister?
> *Sec. Witch,* Killing swine
> *Third Witch,* Sister, Where thou?
> *First Witch,* A sailor's wife had chestnuts in her lap
> And munched and munched and munched; 'Give me,'
> quoth I
> Aroint thee, witch, the rump-fed roynon cries.
> Her husband's to Aleppo gone, master of the Tiger,
> But in a sieve I'll thither sail
> And like a rat without a tail
> I'll do, and I'll do, and I'll do. (1.iii.1-12).

In this text, the witches are depicted as village witches since they attacked the aforementioned pig and another witch asks for food but is refused. As a result the sailor's wife replies with 'Aroint thee' which is not a common phrase to use. She uses supernatural spoken language like any other witches since she knows where the husband's ship sails. That can be seen as evidence that she is truly a witch because witches, as Rosen notes, were believed to wreck ships by creating storms. She gives the case of the King Majesty's ship that had a bad wind suffered a confused journey. Rosen's argument shows us that village witches existed in early England and that is why Shakespeare used the idea of this village witch in *Macbeth*. As told in Matthew, Mark, and Luke, Tolman argues that 'killing swine' and 'sailing in a sieve' "were believed to be common occupations among witches; probably the first of these opinions sprang from the account of the destruction of the herd of swine by the 'devils' and was felt to have some degree of Scriptural authority" (212).

The first witch turned into evil as a result of being refused for the chestnuts by the sailor's wife which is one of the kind of village witch to do evils as a result of other people's failure to give.

This chapter has analyzed the village-witch discourse and elite discourse in early modern England by considering some dramas. That the idea of each plays: The *Witch, The Witch of Edmonton* and *Macbeth* are drawn from the idea of popular beliefs but Doctor Faustus as speculations of philosophy can be looked at as a learned belief of witchcraft. In *Macbeth*, the witches are in fact a reflective figure of the English village witch. Traditional belief in malevolent witches was a familiar one among the peasants in contrast to the diabolical witches. Lady Macbeth tries to acquire a magic power, as a village witch, through her maternal power to harm others, and she misdirects her malevolent maternal power and fill it in with demonic thought instead. Shakespeare more concerned about village level which is rooted from the tensions among the women of peasants whom people believed that they bring back death and sickness to their neighbours.

In *The Witch*, the idea of witchcraft in this play has been drawn from popular belief, when the cunning women casting spells and works for charm, as a subject matter for satire on human wickedness. Similar to Middleton's *The Witch, The Witch of Edmonton*, begins with the high ranked characters from respectable society, i.e. English farmers and country gentlemen but their difficulties and troubles in life leads them to devilish world of witchcraft. However, the witch character takes the lower position in the play. Elizabeth Sawyer was showed as the power of an old woman in the village of Edmonton who did a real harm and she acted as a village witch not elite. Except *Doctor Faustus* which is drawn from an elite magic but one thing belongs him to the popular magic since Faustus thinks of Helen as another succubus when Mephistopheles offered him.

According to popular belief that witches used kiss as a means of doing their magic and wickedness toward others. Kiss in the witch context might relate to the belief that witches pass on their familiar to somebody else through a kiss before they pass away. So, the kiss of Doctor Faustus is the bodily intercourse with Helen, "spirits", and it is the ultimate signal of sin of demoniality. This is similar to Mother Sawyer's teat when she offered to her familiar. Faustus and Sawyer, both had familiar and made a pact with the devil and each of whom has to consider repentance after a pact. This seems to be an element shared by both popular and elite discourses of witchcraft.

CHAPTER THREE

WITCHCRAFT AND GENDER

Gender relations and the social position of women in early modern England contributed to witch trials which saw a great number of spinsters and widows being intimidated within a society which was based on patriarchal family units. Christina Larner in her essay, *"Was Witchcraft-Hunting Women-Hunting?"*, highlights the stereotypical witch as "an independent adult women who does not conform to the male idea of proper female behaviour. She is assertive; she does not require or give love (although she may enchant); she does not nurture men or children, nor care for the weak. She has the power of words- to defend herself or to curse". And "the identification of any women as a witch will, therefore, set against her not only males, but also conforming females and their children" (274). Larner argues that the ratio of females against males in trials for witchcraft reinforces the theory that witch-hunts were part of a sex war. She states that when the witch-hunting is seen in a criminal context, the central idea is the use of authority to terrorize and intimidate women against further strengthening their social standing in the sixteenth and seventeenth centuries.

It has been suggested that witch trials of that period were a strategical campaign to Christianize the countryside and erect an increasingly patriarchal society and culture at that time. Women prosecuted in this campaign were for a large part the victims of suppression in women's history. They were punished for witchcraft and for adultery by their husbands and by those in authority. So witch-hunts and prosecution were gender related especially in terms of making the laws of the trials which the trials focus on which obviously affects women more than men. That is why some agree that witch-hunting is merely a close relative to women hunting.

Witchcraft can be defined as a women's experience under a patriarchal community. Witch prosecution has different interpretations according to critics, Thompson points out the central distinction between "the *theological* interpretation of the crime, with its diabolical covenant and black Sabbats, and the *folkloric* interpretation, with its magic *maleficium*, wreaking vengeance on the children or the cattle or the property of unhelpful neighbours" (308). The idea of witchcraft might have sprung from certain traditional fears and behaviours rather than hypothesises about the gender of evil. Most of the alleged witches were identified as witches instead of women in the trials. Some people relate this to the women's frailty while others thought that witch-hunting officials were hunting witches, not women, without regard to their gender. If they had considered gender norms, they would not prosecute men which components a great ratio in witch-hunting and prosecution. So the focus here seems not to be on the conflict between the sexes but on who the alleged witch threatened and who is considered as the target of evildoing.

Sawyer has focused on belief in witchcraft by looking at the works of Hugh Trevor-Roper as an expression of the "mental rubbish of peasant credulity and feminine hysteria" (461). Sawyer also distinguishes between English witchcraft beliefs and prosecutions from continental in which neither are witches "riding brooms, nor kissing the devil's behind, nor cannibalizing babies – but simple maleficium characterized in English witchcraft" (461). According to witchcraft evidence, witches were both male and female but the most acute focus is on female witches, especially in English studies. This is as a result of "complex economic and social forces as well as traditional folk and Christian beliefs that emphasized the threatening nature of women" (Sawyer 465).

Social interaction between villagers engendered witchcraft accusations and sex and age were also important factors in this area. This is because most of the accused witches were between the ages of forty and sixty. Marine Hester, in her essay, "*Patriarchal Reconstruction and Witch-Hunting*", draws on the idea of Monter that "the accusation of women was not merely a reflection of an age-old stereotype, nor merely the by-product of a patriarchal society; the witch-hunts were a part of, and one example of, the ongoing mechanisms for social control of women within the general context of social change and the reconstruction of a patriarchal society" (276). In the sixteenth and seventeenth centuries there was a powerful attempt to control sexual behaviour of women in particular through accusations of witchcraft. There was a strong belief that women possessed a sexual power in relation to witchcraft. The witches were mostly older women as Hall stresses, by drawing on Thomas's idea of witches as being more vulnerable and were "the most dependent members of the community", so as to evoke "the "old tradition of mutual charity and help" and thus to provoke "the guilt and tensions" that found release in accusations of witchcraft"

(274). In seventeenth century New England, most women held the position of spiritual leader in their household and this threatened men's dominance in the community. As they could practise folk fortune-telling and healing and were marginal and deviant in terms of sexual behaviour, and in social or economic respects.

Favret-Saada states that "the accused sometimes appear as strong beings because they are weak (for instance, blasphemers or witches who cast evil spells because they are incapable of direct physical violence)"; and sometimes the accused appear as weak "because they are strong beings victims of repression because of their rebellion against the patriarchal order, or because they alone have the capacity to give birth, or because men fear menstruation" (574). There is still doubt about the power that witches and magicians have to do harm or perform their tricks, whether they get this hidden power internally or where it is externally acquired. This power is mysterious and harmful according to popular belief, which women and men share, and creates the concept of witchcraft which then comes into certain women. Most witches and victims were neighbours accusations can be domestically explained: one woman might be asked for something or for some friendly service which her neighbour refused and thus a dispute arose where one shows her anger and this behaviour led to her being seen as a witch. It is normally female pronouns which have been used in relation descriptions of a typical witch because in most cases the persons of using witchcraft were woman.

Simpson argues that contemporary commentators are aware of the preponderance of female witches since women were believed to be more easily tempted to sin than men. By drawing on Larner's point of view, Simpson argues this might be related to their femininity in terms of early beliefs considered as "scientific opinion from Pliny onwards which held that menstrual blood could harm crops, food and kill bees, and so on, which made it easy to slip into thinking that there was some form of dangerous magic inherent in all women" (7). This idea made it clear that women's powers were hereditary in particular in the female line and the animal familiars. It is also possible to view this in terms of a religious approach because in this light woman has been seen as a morally weak and that is why she was more easily deceived by Satan. Furthermore, Simpson, looks at witchcraft in relations to gender and by drawing on the ideas of the critics Quaife and Levack, argues that "internationally, it has usually been seen as an echo of religious stereotyping of women as morally weak, credulous and lustful" and "their tasks as cooks, healers, and midwives" easily led to suspicion of using magic" (8). Moreover, most of the women, "especially spinsters and widows", might be accused of witchcraft since they were economically independent and dealt with life on their own by crafts such as brewing, weaving and so on.

Simpson quotes Karlsen's view on the issues of witchcraft and gender that "in America most accused women were not under the control of male relatives and were, or were about to become, independent; they were usually above childbearing age, and in several cases had broken gender norms by sexual misbehaviour, by pride, or by unusual religious views" (8). Women witches were mostly charged with malevolent cursing but men witches were hardly ever accused of being malevolent. Sometimes the alleged witch and the accuser both were women and in terms of gender norms the accusers were also seen as guilty and were like the witches themselves. Therefore, it should not be merely said witch-hunting means women hunting because a minority of men also were also the victims of witchcraft. Women were prosecuted for prostitution, witchcraft and infanticide. Their prosecution was because witchcraft was against the religious and moral code of the government. Larner illustrates that the purpose of a witch-hunt was "the prising out of dangerous persons who were enemies of God, the state and the people" (275). At village level, the accusation of witchcraft was between a woman and the one who alleged she was a witch, i.e. often two women.

In terms of gender, witchcraft was used as a weapon to subordinate women and as a form of sexual violence against women in witchcraft trials. This is because some of the alleged witches, as was pointed out in some trials, had tempted close relatives to incest and others might have had relationships with the same sex. Witch-persecutions can be seen as an attack against independent women by their patriarchal society in which woman has always been cast as inferior to men. Thus, most of the executed witches were women. And, many scholars view the term "witch" merely as woman since they show the witches' trial, executions and crimes. Marine Hester draws on the idea of Thomas that the accused were usually older, poor and often widowed women? Hester argues that

> during the last Tudor and early Stuart period, when formal accusations of witchcraft were at their height, village conflicts around neighbourliness grew especially acute. The erosion of the manorial system with lots of customary tenancies and common land created poverty while at the same time breaking up old cooperative village communities. Widows were particularly adversely affected by the these changes leaving them vulnerable to witchcraft accusation (277).

Women were accused of witchcraft as according to later allegation witchcraft some of the women because of doing their real activities but some of them only by the beliefs of ordinary people of which their association with their alleged victims. Their accusations and trial centred upon the belief that a witch could harm the health of humans and of animals; and suckle teats, animal familiars and certain marks all were supposedly mentioned in the witch trials but very rarely did magical flight and transformations feature (Simpson 6).

Witch prosecutions were usually a war between similars: woman and woman, i.e. the witch and the accuser. Both were female and participated in criminal persecution. Holmes identifies three groups of women who participated in the trial procedures against women thus: the first group are those who were "the "possessed" victims of the witch's malice; control of their mind and body had been seized by the Devil at the instigation of the witch." The second group are those reporting "the results of physical searches that they hade been instructed to conduct upon the witch's body, designed to discover the incriminating physical characteristics that indicated her complicity with Satan and his minions." The third group are those who were "testified simply to their experience of the witch's maleficium- to children lamed or killed, to stock or crops blighted, to the interruption of agricultural or domestic procedures" (45-46). The last one seems to be more based on traditional belief rather than elite belief. In the early sixteenth century women were centrally involved in witchcraft accusation and they did witness against the alleged witches. Holmes confirms that during Elizabeth's reign (1596-1602) 38.2 per cent witnesses against witches were women and 43.4 per cent in the reign of James I, but after the Restoration this rate increased to 52.9 per cent in the counties which formed the Home Circuit (48). This shows that the perception of the nature of witchcraft among people increased became more and more and it was considered to be a criminal offence and an indictment. However, with the instigation of the legal elite this perception lessoned except in the cases where illness led to death or in case of diabolic practices.

exclusively prone to accusations of witchcraft and magic practises: some men were also targets of witchcraft accusations but the majority of the accused were women. That is why in early modern England witchcraft accusation is a concept tied to femaleness rather than maleness. Gender norms contributed to the preponderance of females among the accused at that time since women tended to be at home and their activities limited within a certain circle of neighbours, relatives and people around themselves. However, men's magical activities were not constrained in one location but changed from place to place: in military bases, in the taverns and etc. Goodare points out that witch-hunts in Scotland lasted from about (1550) to (1700) and were mainly directed at women. While most recorded crimes were committed by males: three witches in twenty were males (289). Goodare also argues that the "typical witch was not only female: she was poor. But most folk in early modern Scotland were poor, and she was not usually much poorer than her neighbours" (290). The witch-hunters were men, they were lairds and sheriffs of the peace, who arrested and interrogated the suspected witches. Goodare illustrates a good point in which he shows why women were an easy target of witchcraft accusations especially between the late sixteenth century to the early seventeenth century. In that period many Scotsmen migrated to the continent as mercenary soldiers, nearly 35,000 of whom never returned. So this increased poverty levels and led to many women being deprived of present and future marriage partners so they became poor also and lacked male protection (292). Thus, witches might have been old women and widows because of the poverty situation of that time. Moreover, women became scapegoats in the processes of the witch-hunts since they were a part of the economic problem, and that meant women could easily find themselves in court more than men for any poverty-related reason. Witches were old women and therefore had no role as nurturing mother so this could lead to quarrels and rivalries over mothering issues. Goodare examines the sexual relations between the Devil and the witch in which "women were usually free to draw upon their imaginations when interrogated about the details of their sexual relationship with the devil, as long as they did confess to it, of course". Most witches gave a brief and perfunctory description which revealed it had been unpleasant and could hardly have been enjoyable (295).

Although men were also involved in witchcraft alongside women they could sometimes escape prosecution. The male witch was like the female witch: they did what the woman witch did but less dramatically. They also confessed to have had the Devil's mark as women. However, one thing which distinguishes the male witch from the female one is that they did not confess to having sexual relationships with the Devil. They did not seal the demonic pact with the Devil by sexual intercourse but the female witches did and what they always wanted and which distinguished them from the female witches was submissiveness. However, the female witches openly displayed malice. They seemed more as male healers than witches and they had also a baton as a symbol of weapon and power over women and witches but the female witches had a shear or sieve. Male witches were always a minor target for witch prosecutions and for the authorities. There may be other, further reasons why women became witches besides those which have been discussed here, for example uncontrolled sexuality and the fear of curses and other factors which may have lead individuals to witchcraft.

In *The Witch of Edmonton*, three writers dramatise the conflicts of both social and demonic power in the tiny rural town of Edmonton near London. The double actions of the witch of Edmonton give structural unity to the play through the theme of the knowledge of both good and evil. Elizabeth Sawyer is seen as a product of her society rather than being anomalous in it as she points out that she lacks any knowledge of witchcraft and was only taught by her neighbours unintentionally:

> "Some call me a witch,
> And, being ignorant of myself, they go
> About to teach me how to be done, urging
> That my bad tongue, by their bad usage made so,
> Forespeaks their cattle, doth bewitch their corn,
> Themselves, their servants and their babes at nurse.
> (Ii.i.8-15)

Through her speeches, Sawyer proves that she is not a witch since she does not have any knowledge of good or evil on witchcraft but falls into witchcraft through temptations and ignorance. Corbin and Sedge consider this opening soliloquy of Sawyer by which the audience is invited to "respond to her with sympathy as a victim both of the devil's wiles and the social prejudices of the community in which she lives"; and they agree that it was society which predisposes women to behave and feel in ways which expose them to the devil's temptation, if it does not exactly make them witches (24-25). She acknowledged that she had a bad tongue as a result of the ill-treatment of the villagers toward her. Her society constructed her gender identity as a witch. While she blames her neighbours and says:

> Still vexed? still tortured? That Curmudgeon Banks,
> Is ground of all my scandal. I am shunned
> And hated like a sickness: made a scorn
> To all degrees and sexes. I have heard old Beldams
> Talk of Familiars in the shape of Mice,
> Rats, Ferrets, Weasels, and I wot not what,

That have appeared, and sucked, some say, their
blood.
But by what means they came acquainted with them,
I'm now ignorant: would some power good or bad,
Instruct me which way I might be revenged
Upon this Churl, I'd go out of my self
And give this Fury leave to dwell within
This ruined Cottage, ready to fall with age,
Abjure all goodness: be at hate with prayer,
And study Curses, Imprecations,
Blasphemous speeches, Oaths, detested Oaths,
Or any thing that's ill; so I might work
Revenge upon this Miser, this black Cur
That barks, and bites, and sucks the very blood
Of me and of my credit. 'Tis all one
To be a Witch, as to be counted one.
Vengeance, shame, ruin, light upon that Canker!
(II.i.98-120).

This shows the reader mother Sawyer's understandable anger who has been abused and beaten by her own surroundings. This leads her to desire and revenge herself by provoking her dog, her familiar, to appear and make a pact with the Devil. She is entrapped into the world of witchcraft, when the devil threatens her to tear her body into a thousands pieces, rather than as a wicked criminal looking to achieve a devilish power. She shows herself as ignorant that she does not have any knowledge of this devilish power whether it would be good or bad. She is a victim of both the social prejudice of her village in one hand, and the devil on the other hand. This can be analyzed in gender discourse as, because of the fact she is an old, poor and isolated woman, she is abused by her community and seen as a witch.

The gender discourse has been mapped comprehensibly in Marlowe's *Doctor Faustus* especially in terms of gender subjectivity. Marlowe allures the reader with the dramatizing of the figure of an unrepentant sinner who would not repent and save his soul as a magician as having a lack of right track to direct his will. He always tried to get out of the pact with Lucifer and was not free to achieve salvation. This is merely a reflection of the position of a rebellious man and his destiny according to a traditional orthodox Christian point of view. Hill further highlights the orthodoxy of Doctor Faustus by which it hardly stands in need of "background" support. However, "a useful result of analyzing relationship to the morality tradition is to show the differences within superficial likeness, according due honour to the sophistication of Marlowe's art" (310-311). Faustus's role has been shown as a life of a blasphemous man which is movingly tragic and turns his insatiable curiosity into black magic.

The masculinity of the two heroes in *Macbeth* and *Doctor Faustus* are to some extent similar: Macbeth from the beginning of the play was a noble man and an excellent warrior. However, when he succumbed to the temptation of seeking power by killing Duncan, his path was turned steeply downward and he became a callous murderer. Similar to Doctor Faustus, his intellectual power, in the black magic role, dissipates into trivial show and sensuality. Birringer stresses the hallucinatory quality of Faustus's visions and the agony of the moment which grows into a torrent of concentrated language. This presents the audience with the tough mission of assimilating the opposite voices of the psychically and physically divided man (354).

> O Ile leape vp to my God: who pulles me downe?
> See see where Christs blood streames in the firmament,

One drop would saue my soule, halfe a drop, ah my
Christ,
Ah rend not my heart for naming of my Christ,
Yet wil I call on him, oh spare me Lucifer!
Where is it now? tis gone. [A. 1462-1467]

Ornstein stresses this comparison further showing that Macbeth's
fall increasingly isolates him from his fellowmen. However, Faustus'
fall was a "means of communication with others and at least he
was surrounded by others who pray and protect him from the devil,
but Faustus will not allow them to risk their lives and souls for him"
(1382). Birringer stressed another similarity between Macbeth and
Faustus: when Faustus is dreaming about his damnation, ""the
written troubled of the brain" as Macbeth calls it before he learns
the wood is moving toward Dunsinane- is dramatically transformed
into a more literal spectacle: The Devils will come, they will hold
him" (351).

> Lucif. Thus from infemall Dis do we ascend
> To view the subiects of our Monarchy,
> Those soules which sinne, seales the blacke
>   sonnes of hell,
> 'Mongw hich as chiefe, Faustusw e come to
>   thee,
> Bringingw ith vs lastingd amnation [B.
>   1895-1899]

One can see much semantic opposition in Faustus's damnation
such as God and Devil, theology and blasphemy and sainthood with
rebellion. He wants to get rid of the doctrinal world through his
"magic" power but could not succeed. The relationship between

language and body is the core of the theatre, most strikingly in plays where body acts as language to present tragedy or comedy in which the characters protect themselves from the delusion of death. In *The Witch of Middleton*, Elizabeth Sawyer acts as an alleged bad witch, Faustus in *Doctor Faustus* plays a tragic role of a blasphemous magician, in *Macbeth*, Lady Macbeth as a malevolent mother of early modern England: all these represent a meaningful acts in the patriarchal societies of early modern England and show how the body in performance is a result of the textural relations between the events of the play.

In contrast to Elizabeth Sawyer, in *The Witch of Edmonton*, the witches in *The Witch*, are presented as less obnoxious than the human characters of the play. Mother Sawyer from the beginning of the play, sympathetically shows herself to the reader as a disempowered old woman who becomes a witch in order to retaliate against her enemies in the village of Edmonton. Mother Sawyer could successful become a malicious witch since she was able to cause death and attack her enemies. In contrast to Mother Sawyer, the witches in *The Witch* are presented to show the society's neurosis surrounding female chastity in a patriarchal society. For example, Hecate with her fellow witches had not enough time for chastity and they walked around at night to meet young men. However, in the case of Hecate not finding anyone suitable, she would make do with Fireston, her son, or even with Malkin, her cat, rather than going without sex. Purkiss states that these numerous sexual transgressions in *The Witch* which more than anything unite the witch-plot and main plot are similarly decorative. She further stresses Hecate's power "to dry up generation ought to be a serious threat, as should her incestuous relationship with her son, but no frisson of real fear or disorder attends these revelations as Middelton represents them" (219).

The witches' promiscuity, in *The Witch*, is censured and condemned by the play itself and is shown to be repulsive and abided for the cult of female chastity and women's sexuality by the norms of a patriarchal society. Most of the lines of this play are covered by the queries of female chastity among the characters. For example, in order to hide the loss of her virginity, Francisca turns to killing through a proxy; Isabella's hymen should have been broken by Antonio, but this was prevented from happening by Sebastian, by the casting of a spell from Hecate. The Duchess is another woman figure who tried to clear her sin of unchastity and was loved to be executed as killer. We could say that Middelton has put a survey of all traditional female roles into his play: e.g. witch, widow, prostitute, wife, and unmarried woman. The male characters in the play in association to the female chastity are shown in a bad light through the cases of Antonio, Sebastian and Almachildes. Almachildes complains that the woman had deceived him when he realized that the woman who he wanted to deflower did not have an intact hymen: "This's you that was a maid? How are you born/ To deceive men! I'd thought to have married you; / I had been finely handled, had I not? / I'll say that man is wise ever hereafter/ That tries his wife beforehand. 'Tis no marvel/ You should profess such bashfulness to blind one" (iii.i.16). Sebastian also considered as his own right when he wanted to rape Isabella but then he changed his mind. Unlike other Jacobean plays, the characters, and the witches, in *The Witch* are not punished or tried, although they show the witches' attempts to carry out their criminal acts. There are some scenes that show the high ranking authorities let the sinners go unpunished and get away with killing: "That with a beck can suppress multitudes, / And dim misdeeds with radiance of his glory, / Not to be seen with dazzled, popular eyes" (iv.i.51-53) and "That woman that, unworthy, wears your blood / To countenance sin in her – your niece – she's false" (v.i.93-94). However, one of the few characters, who did not use the witches and fell down, was Antonio: while the others were pardoned. The differences between genders here have been constructed and through these differences, the essentialness of gender is reinforced.

Similarly to *The Witch*, in *Macbeth*, feminine power dominates masculine power in cases where: witches, wives, mothers are endowed with the same nightmarish powers through both magical and nonmagical means, Willis says. Using these powers "they manipulate men and make them feel as if they are dependent and powerless children" (8). Maternal danger in *Macbeth* constructs or strengthens the theme of witchcraft and makes it more the object of legal prosecution. Through some texts in *Macbeth*, Shakespeare makes his reader conjure up the importance of gender in early English witchcraft. Drawing on Butler's theorization of gender as performative, Salih argues that gender has neither origin nor cause but it is "an open-ended process, a sequence of acts or events which does not originate and which is never fully or finally "realized"" (90). Salih also points out that according to Butler's theorization of gender, casting gender in terms of "performativity" is implied in linguistic and discursive terms rather than having a piece of theatre staged by a knowing actor who selects his/her script at will. In *Macbeth*, the characters identify their gender though their roles or acts which is apparent from the language they use. Lady Macbeth through her acts as a malevolent mother figure chooses her gender, not through her being. Butler argues that "if gender is a "doing" rather than a "being," a verb rather than a noun, it is not an action that is done by a volitional agent who is free to select her/his gender "style"" (qtd. in Salih 91). The gender role of the characters, the witches, Lady Macbeth and Macbeth in *Macbeth* is ambiguous. The witches' gender is ambiguous because of their physical appearance but Lady Macbeth and Macbeth select their gender through their acts.

Drawing on the work of Adelman, Chamberlain states that *Macbeth* is about the demonstrations of fears about male identity and control of one's mind. It is Macbeth who kills Duncan with the fatal dagger but "it is Lady Macbeth's infanticidal fantasy prompted by the witches' prophecy which makes possible a succession rendered barren through crass cruelty and emotional depravity" (83).

In *The Witch of Edmonton*, Mother Sawyer's identity as witch is constituted by her society because in the beginning of the play she was not a witch but she turned to witchcraft since she was abused and insulted the villagers. In Marlowe's *Doctor Faustus*, Doctor Faustus's identity is also constituted as a magician since he tried to find the hidden and secret knowledge of nature. However, the gender identity of the Three Sisters, and Hecate in both plays *Macbeth* and *The Witch* are represented to the reader as witches. Their gender identity is selected as witches through their evil acts.

Macbeth is more about the relationship between gender and power and the witchcraft element is used to explore these ideas. Witches as malevolent mothers use their power to suckle, feed and nourish small demons as though they were children due to bring death and sickness to the other mothers. Witches are always known to be bad mothers and are known to harm and bring sickness and death to others. Purkiss points out that anxiety about a "maternal power which would replace the mother's own role displaced into anxieties about relations between a deformed maternity and a paternity that would be autotelic." (213). Lady Macbeth's mother role is an example of a case of maternal anxieties in early modern times where her role shows a relation between a deformed maternity and an autotelic paternity. She plays the masculine role in the play since she prepares herself for the deed to kill Duncan by Macbeth by asking the spirit to change and "unsex" her. Bernstein points out Lady Macbeth "overpowered Macbeth, not in physical strength, but by subtle manipulation" (34). As a case of many early modern infanticidal mothers she seemed to be a monstrous being. After having given some examples, Chamberlain argues that the infanticidal mothers in early modern times are all like Lady Macbeths, "who would lightly dash out the brains of the babes entrusted to their care" (77). He also points out that the existing early modern anxieties about the infanticidal mother are about "the inherent dangers of maternal agency both to helpless children as well as to a patrilineal system dependent upon woman for its perpetuation" (77). However, Lady Macbeth's infanticidal mother role is merely to be a queen and not to allow Duncan's patrilineal system to continue. Her hysterical situation can be seen as a transformation from a demonic matriarch, witch, into the hysteric, the benign mother. Levin argues that Lady Macbeth resists a "splitting of the demonic matriarch and the secular mother, and her narrative development figure shows the many continuities between the witch and the hysteric" (38).

Shakespeare makes his reader doubt the gender role of the characters, Lady Macbeth and Macbeth. By showing the images of the Weird Sisters and Lady Macbeth, the audience has ideas of both masculine and feminine that are complicated. This is very clear when Lady Macbeth manipulates Macbeth by questioning his manhood: when Macbeth has doubts about killing Duncan, Lady Macbeth questions his manhood by calling him coward: "When you durst do it, then you were a man" (i.vii.49). Kahn argues that Macbeth is taunted by his wife about his cowardice "by holding up a verbal picture of herself as a nursing mother who, precisely at the height of trusting intimacy between her child and herself, would not scruple to snatch her nipple away and dash the brain out" (37):

> I have given suck, and know
> How tender 'tis to love the babe that milks me

> I would, while it was smiling in my face,
> Have plucked my nipple from his boneless gums
> And dashed the brains out, had I sworn
> As you have done to this. (I.Vii. 54-59).

Lady Macbeth's image or role here is changed from a caring or nurturing mother to an infanticidal one since she wants to divest all of the vestiges of her womanliness. She is a representative of, as Cakebread notes, "a shift from the passive 'milky' masculinity she associates with the weak men in the play to a power position which resonates with a sense of maternal evil"(12). Lady Macbeth is thinking of killing the babe when he is smiling in her face. In addition, Lady Macbeth also can be seen as male gendered when she asks the spirit to "unsex" her and exchange the milk of her breast for gall. Chamberlain notes that Lady Macbeth appears as a case familiar to many of the early modern nursing mothers when her milk turns to gall harming the innocent entrusted to her care. Lady Macbeth challenges Macbeth's masculinity and she violates the gender hierarchy. She is trying to catapult herself into the position of power over Macbeth.

Willis argues that the witch's gender is suggested by the "witch stereotype itself, which associates the practise of harmful magic with misdirected nurture" and it is regarded as a symbolic malevolent anti-mother to her neighbours and their children by the villagers since she brings sickness and death to the other mothers (33). Furthermore, she points out that witches are not biologically considered as female by popular belief but instead they represent it in terms of maternal figure. Witches are confirmed as female by having a teat which they use as a means for gaining demonic power. Lady Macbeth uses her breast as a mark to prove that she acquires demonic power by calling the spirit to carry out what she is trying for. As a malevolent mother- figure, Lady Macbeth uses her power to take away her human kindness and fill her breast with thoughts of murder. These murderous thoughts of Lady Macbeth cause her to push Macbeth to murder. However his anxiety and guilt becomes too much when he kills Duncan. He exclaims "What hands are here? Ha! They pluck out mine eyes" (ii.ii.65). Drawing on the idea of the critic Adelman, Levin argues that Lady Macbeth's calling on the spirit may not be asking them to change her milk for gall as much as she instructs them to take her milk as gall. Lady Macbeth might show us an image of devil worshiping since she invites them and offers them her reproductive abilities in exchange for their demonic power. Her role as hysterical mother in the play represents "a split within the mother figure in patriarchy and, in particular, point to tensions between maternity and female autonomy, between procreation and sexuality, and between nurture and reproductive capability" (Levin 38). Lady Macbeth's hysteria is interpreted as a case of involvement with witchcraft. When Lady Macbeth becomes hysterical, the doctor says: "this disease is beyond my practice: yet I have known those which have walked in their sleep, who have died holily in their bed" (v.i.55-57).The doctor's speech proves that she needs a spiritual remedy rather than a physical one. The sleep walking shows her guilty conscience and Shakespeare portrays her as a sinner who tries to wash away her sin.

In early modern England women were accused for being witches through their mental delusions such as melancholy or hysteria. Or it might have been because of their mental trickery caused by scheming devils in female minds. A demonic action is always deemed to be against Divine actions and a female's power to be against their godly male authority. Witches were accused to have committed many murders such as the slaughter of animals, killing through giving poison or harming children and/or infanticide and somehow having relations with the devil. In early modern England women did not only have the position of caring mother to fill but also that of malevolent mother. *Macbeth* shows us that during Shakespearean times, witches were not the only sources of threat to the patriarchal order and could convince men to act in their own interests. However, the image of the infanticidal mother is also another source showing witches to be a threat to men and patriarchal authority. Lady Macbeth's temptation goads Macbeth on to many killings and then his own terror which highlights that all Macbeth's weak masculinity stems from his wife's maternal imagination. However, at the end of the play, Lady Macbeth is trying to recuperate and create her femininity again in her somnambulism while she says:

> "Come, come, come, give me your hand: What's done cannot be undone: To bed, to bed, to bed." (v. i. 61-63).

Her somnambulism can be defined as a psychic meaning of gendered presentation since her situation can not be explained and treated by a natural remedy. She needs a spiritual remedy rather than a physical one. In applying the performative gender theory of Butler to this play, Lady Macbeth's hysteria can be analyzed in terms of the gender problem through understanding performative theories, linguistically and casting her theatrically. When Lady Macbeth performs repetitive language, theatrically, the audience interpret her words differently. She might be seen as a real witch, a malevolent mother figure, a village witch or she might not be. However, linguistically, the words she uses are related to her body gestures. She selects her gender through her acts not through her being. This shows that there is no originality for gender identity, as Butler says, but it is performatively constituted. Butler argues "there is no "being" behind doing, acting, becoming; "the doer" is merely a fiction imposed on the doing - the doing itself is everything" (qtd in Salih 104). Lady Macbeth constitutes her identity as a malevolent mother figure as a result of divesting and refusing her femininity not because of the fact that she is a female character. So "there is no gender identity behind the expressions of gender; ... identity is performatively constituted by the very "expressions" that are said to be its results." (qtd. in Salih 104). By giving the image of Lady Macbeth, the reader sees the problem of gender politics of the past time. In other words, Lady Macbeth kills herself to show that at that time women had no right to overcome men in patriarchal society. Shakespeare gave Lady Macbeth such a role that her life should be ended at the end of the play. Her remorse drives her to kill herself and to reverse the idea that she is not a witch, if she is, she should not have killed herself. Witches did not show remorse and kill themselves if they had harmed others in early England. That is why the play makes her pay for her rebellious behaviour by killing herself.

The witches of the other aforementioned Renaissance dramas also came to their fates by the end of the plays. In *The Witch of Middleton*, Elizabeth Sawyer was ostracized by her neighbours and like the other convicted witches she emerged as a rebel and her life came to an end. Although one can not find any definite evidence of Doctor Faustus's fate, in *Marlowe's Doctor Faustus*, but his clothes were seen by his friends which were strewn about the stage in the final confrontation with Mephistophilis in the later "B" text of the play. In contrast to the three mentioned dramas, Middleton's *The Witch* is not about a witch's trial and execution in the witch-hunts. Instead, it shows the reader the comical singing of the witches who are never in any fear of being brought to trial and tortured. The characters are not punished or tried to punish although they attempt to carry out criminal acts. There are some scenes that show

CONCLUSION

The first chapter has analyzed the general overview of witchcraft history in early modern England which emerged in the later middle Ages in the era when the concept of sorcery was transformed to witchcraft. Witchcraft was rooted in sorcery and witches were not merely sorcerers but they had also interaction with demonic powers and added on some diabolical flourishes. One comes to the point that the idea of witchcraft sprang from human experience within specific cultural arenas, instead of prosecuting dogma in one hand and community scapegoating on the other. The elite and the popular are two different dynamic components of witchcraft but not rival definitions of witchcraft. Belief in witchcraft was endemic and rooted in society's beliefs and did not vanish with the emergence and rise of science; and it was socially functional and real and could be viewed as social interaction among the villagers as a result of sporadic conflicts among themselves.

Witchcraft as a power emerging between the witch and Satan, in popular belief, was actually trivial and crude power. Magicians and witches always were condemned for their tricks and demonic acts. The first chapter has illustrated that witchcraft has been used differently by the dramatists who claimed to approach the social history of their community. Some of them were about witch trials and others about witch-hunts. For example, Shakespeare's *Macbeth* has focused more on the witch's power to shape the man's destiny; *The Witch of Edmonton* was about notorious trials. However, Middleton's *The Witch* was not about a witch's trial and execution in the witch-hunts. Instead, it was about the comical singing of the witches who are never in any fear of being brought to trial and being tortured. Moreover, it shows how the witches tried to satisfy their own lusts by sleeping with visitors, succubi and their own offspring. The witch scenes in *The Witch* condemn the corrupt society of early modern England instead of centring on individuals. Unlike the three aforementioned plays, Christopher Marlowe's *Doctor Faustus* is mentioned as being more about natural magic when the magician tries to reveal some hidden or secret things in nature, while the works of nature themselves or the seeking of natural power is associated with bewitchment and the world of witchcraft. Faustus in his career tried to escape from the human condition through performing similar acts on Christ. Doctor Faustus signed a pact with the devil to commit a sin of demoniality without repenting. Faustus tells his audience that he damned himself in a conventional way which finally ended up with his self-destruction.

In the second chapter, I have centred on the two different types of witches, village and elite. The village level is thought to be rooted in the tensions among women peasants when people believed that witches could bring death and sickness on their neighbours. The village witches practised the theory of *maleficium* to do harm to their neighbours. However, the elite were believed according to other theories of witchcraft to be having a sexual pact with the Devil. Shakespeare's *Macbeth*, *The Witch* and *The Witch of Edmonton*, the idea of witchcraft in three of them is drawn from that typified by the village level witchcraft. In contrast, Marlowe's *Doctor Faustus*, has its idea drawn from elite discourse of witchcraft. In these plays, the witch characters signed a pact with the Devil and afterwards had to consider repentance. It is clearly shown that considering repentance after such a pact is an element shared by both village and elite discourses of witchcraft.

The third chapter of this study has illustrated the association of witchcraft with gender in early England through analysing the texts of the plays. This chapter has examined how gender relations in early England contributed to witch trials and witch prosecutions as women were clearly victimised by that particular campaign in women's history. Witchcraft has been defined as a women's experience under a patriarchal community and witch-hunting has been compared to women hunting although there were also male victims. Witch-hunts, in the sixteenth and seventeenth centuries, victimised women using the term "witches" and focussed on old women, spinsters and widows. Women alone were not prone to accusations of using witchcraft and magic practises, but there were men who were also targets of witchcraft accusations, but the majority of the accused were women. That is why in early modern England witchcraft accusations are mostly tied to the idea of femaleness. Gender norms contributed to the preponderance of females among the accused at that time since they tended to stay at home and restrict their activities within a certain circle of their neighbours, relatives and people around themselves. However, men's magical activities were not restricted to one place but moved from place to place: e.g. in military bases, in the taverns.

There were other reasons why women were accused more often of witchcraft than men as they were biologically weaker and could not compare in terms of direct aggressions. Therefore, they tended to employ indirect violence through casting spells which could harm their neighbours. Another interpretation has focused on female as victims of witchcraft since they are able to give birth and women's bodies are more easily tempted by Satan. The study has also examined why women witches were charged more often with malevolent cursing, while male witches were rarely accused of being malevolent. Sometimes the alleged witch and the accuser were both women and in terms of gender norms the accusers were also held to be as guilty as the witches were themselves.

BIBLIOGRAPHY

Anderson, Alan and Raymond Gordon. "Witchcraft and the Status of Women". The British Journal of Sociology. 29 (1978):174. JSTOR. Tremough Campus Lib., Penryn. 12th October 2009. < http://www. jstor.org/stable/589887>.

Atkinson, David. "Moral Knowledge and the Double Action in The Witch of Edmonton". Studies in English Literature. 25 (1985): (420, 432, 462). JSTOR. Tremough Campus Lib., Penryn. 18th, August 2009. < http://www.jstor.org/stable/450730>.

Bailey, Michael D. "From Sorcery to Witchcraft: Clerical Conceptions of Magic in the Later Middle Ages". Speculum. 76 (2001): (961, 963-4). JSTOR. Tremough Campus Lib., Penryn. 2nd, August 2009. < http://www.jstor.org/stable/2903617>.

Bernstein, Jane A. "Bewitched, Bothered and Bewildered': Lady Macbeth, Sleepwalking, and the Demonic in Verdi's Scottish Opera". Cambridge Opera Journal. 14 (2002): 34. JSTOR.

Tremough Campus Lib., Penryn. 11th, August 2009. <http//:www. jstor.org/stable/3878281>.

Bever, Edward. "Witchcraft, Female Aggression, and Power in the Early Modern Community". Journal of Social History. 35 (2002): (959, 970). JSTOR. Tremough Campus Lib., Penryn. 2nd, August 2009. <http://www.jstor.org/stable/3790618>.

Bevington, David and Eric Rasmussen. Doctor Faustus A- and B-texts (1604, 1616): Christopher Marlowe and his collaborator and revisers. Manchester and New York: Manchester University Press, 1993.

Birringer, Johannes H. "Between Body and Language: "Writing" the Damnation of Faustus". Theatre Journal. 36 (1984): (338, 351, 354). JSTOR. Tremough Campus Lib., Penryn. 26th, August 2009. <http://www.jstor.org/stable/3206951>.

Bradley, A. C. Shakespearean Tragedy. New York: Palgrave, 1992.

Brink, Jean R., Coudert Allison P., and Horowitz Maryanne C. The Politics of Gender in Early Modern Europe. Ariz: Tempe, 1987.

Brooke, John L. Rev. of "Witchcraft, Magic, and Religion in Seventeenth-Century Massachusetts" ed. By Richard Weisman. Journal of Interdisciplinary History. 16 (1985): 348. JSTOR. Tremough Campus Lib., Penryn. 2nd, August 2009. < http://www. jstor.org/stable/204204>.

Butler, Judith. "Bodily Inscriptions, Performative Subversions". in The Judith Butler Reader. Ed. Sarah Salih. Malden, Oxford, and Carlton: Blackwell, 2004. pp. (90-118).

Cakebread, Caroline. "Macbeth and Feminism". Shakespeare Institute: University of Birmingham. 11-13. <http://bcsd.k12. ny.us/high/lmc/essays.pdf>

Callaghan, Dymphna. Rev. of "Shakespearean Tragedy and Gender" by Shirley Nelson Garner and Madelon Sprengnether. Shakespeare Quarterly. 48 (1997): JSTOR. Tremough Campus Lib., Penryn. 11th, April. 2009. <http//:www.jstor.org/stable/2871285>.

Callaghan, Dymphna. "Wicked Women in Macbeth: A Study of Power, Ideology and the Production of Motherhood" in Mario A. Di Cesare, Reconsidering the Renaissance. Binghampton, New York: Medieval and Renaissance Texts and Studies, 1982. pp(355-393).

Chamberlain, Stephanie. "Fantasizing Infanticide: Lady Macbeth and the murdering Mother in Early Modern England". College Literature. 3 (2005): (77,83) JSTOR. Tremough Campus Lib., Penryn. 20th September. 2009. <http//:www.jstor.org/stable/25115288>.

Clark, Stuart. Thinking with Demons: The Idea of Witchcraft in Early Modern Europe. New York: Oxford University Press, 1997. Colson, Elizabeth. "The Father as Witch". Journal of the International African Institute. 70 (2000): 334. JSTOR. Tremough Campus Lib., Penryn. 2nd, August 2009. < http://www.jstor.org/ stable/1161065>.

Corbin, Peter and Douglas Sedge. Three Jacobean Witchcraft Plays: Sophonisba, The witch and The Witch of Edmonton. Manchester and New York: Palgrave,1986.

Cox, Gerald H. "Marlowe's "Doctor Faustus" and "Sin against the Holy Ghost". The Huntington Library Quarterly.36 (1973): (120, 122, 131). JSTOR. Tremough Campus Lib., Penryn. 26th, August 2009. < http://www.jstor.org/stable/3816592>.

Demos, Putnam John. Entertaining Satan: Witchcraft and the Culture of Early New England. Oxford, New York, Toronto and Melbourne: Oxford University Press, 1982.

Eccles, Mark. "Recent Studies in Elizabethan and Jacobean Drama". Studies in English Literature. 13 (1973): (403-4). JSTOR. Tremough Campus Lib., Penryn. 26th, August 2009. < http://www.jstor.org/stable/449746>.

Favret-Saada, Jeanne. Rev. of "Witchcraft and Religion: The Politics of Popular Belief by". Ed. By Christina Larner. American Ethnologist. 14 (1987): 574. JSTOR. Tremough Campus Lib., Penryn. 2nd, August 2009. < http://www.jstor.org/stable/644971>.

Fuss, Diana J. ""Essentially Speaking": Luce Irigaray's Language of Essence". Hypatia. 3 (1989): 62. JSTOR. Tremough Campus Lib., Penryn. 8th October 2009. <http://www.jstor.org/stable/3809788>.

Gaskill, Malcolm. Rev. of "Witches and Neighbours: The Social and Cultural Context of European Witchcraft" ed. By Briggs and "Instruments of Darkness: Witchcraft in England 1550-1750" ed. By James Sharp. Social History. 23 (1998): 213-214. JSTOR.

Tremough Campus Lib., Penryn. 2nd, August 2009. < http://www.jstor.org/stable/4286492>.

Gilbert, Sandra M. "A Tarentella of Theory Sandra M. Gilbert". Introduction. The Newly Born Woman. Ed. Helen Cixous and Catherine Clement. London: I. B. Tauris and Co Ltd, 1996. http://books.google.co.uk/books?id=hzJHtq6jGHEC&printsec=frontcover &source=gbs v2 summary r&cad=0#v=onepage&q=&f=false

Gibson, Marion. Early Modern Witches: Witchcraft Cases in Contemporary Writing. London and New York: Routledge, 2000.

_____. "Witchcraft and Society in England and America, 1550-1750". London: Continuum, 2003.

_____. Early Modern Witches: Witchcraft Cases in Contemporary Writing. London, New York and Canada: Routledge, 2000. pp (72-125).

Goodare, Julian. "Women and the Witch-Hunt in Scotland". Social History. 23 (1998): (289, 290, 292, 295, 302). JSTOR. Tremough Campus Lib., Penryn. 2nd, August 2009. < http://www.jstor.org/stable/4286516>.

Hale, David G. Rev. of "Malevolent Nurture: Witch-Hunting and Maternal Power in Early Modern England". Ed. By Deborah Willis. Renaissance Quarterly. 50 (1997): 662. JSTOR. Tremough Campus Lib., Penryn. 2nd, August 2009. < http://www.jstor.org/stable/3039250>.

Hall, David D. "Witchcraft and the Limits of Interpretation". The New England Quarterly. 58 (1985): (244, 253, 255). JSTOR. Tremough Campus Lib., Penryn. 2nd, August 2009. < http://www.jstor.org/stable/365516>. Herrington, H. W. "Witchcraft and Magic in the Elizabethan Drama". The Journal of American Folklore. 32 (1919):461. JSTOR. Tremough Campus Lib., Penryn. 18th, August 2009. < http://www.jstor.org/stable/535187>.

Hester, Marianne. "Patriarchal Reconstruction and Witch-Hunting" in Darren Oldridge, The Witch Reader. London and New York: Routledge, 2002. pp. (276-89).

Hill, R. F. Rev. of "Suffering and Evil in the Plays of Christopher Marlowe". Ed. by Douglas Cole. The Review of English Studies. 15 (1964): (310-11). JSTOR. Tremough Campus Lib., Penryn. 26th, August 2009. < http://www.jstor.org/stable/512521>.

Holmes, Clive. "Women: Witnesses and Witches". Past & Present. 140 (1993): (45-6, 48, 58, 65). JSTOR. Tremough Campus Lib., Penryn. 2nd, August 2009. < http://www.jstor.org/stable/651213>.

Howitt, A. W. "On Australian Medicine Men; or, Doctors and Wizards of Some Australian Tribes". The Journal of the Anthropological Institute of Great Britain and Ireland. 16 (1887): 24. JSTOR. Tremough Campus Lib., Penryn. 13th October 2009. < http://www.jstor.org/stable/2841737>

Hunter G. K. "Five-Act Structure in "Doctor Faustus". The Tulane Drama Review. 8 (1964): 84. JSTOR. Tremough Campus Lib., Penryn. 26th, August 2009. < http://www.jstor.org/stable/1124920>.

Hutton, Ronald. "Paganism and Polemic: The Debate over the Origins of Modern Pagan Witchcraft". Folklore. 111 (2000): (104-105). JSTOR. Tremough Campus Lib., Penryn. 13th October 2009. < http://www.jstor.org/stable/1260981>

Kahn, Coppelia. "Magic of bounty": Timon of Athens, Jacobean Patronage, and Maternal Power". Shakespeare Quarterly. 38 (1987): 37. JSTOR. Tremough Campus Lib., Penryn. 10th Oct. 2009. <http//:www.jstor.org/stable/2870400>.

Kiessling, Nicolas. "Doctor Faustus and the Sin of Demoniality". Studies in English Literature. 15 (1975): 211. JSTOR. Tremough Campus Lib., Penryn. 26th, August 2009. < http://www.jstor.org/stable/449667>.

Kivelson, Valerie. "Male Witches and Gendered Categories in Seventeenth-Century Russia". Comparative Studies in Society and History. 45 (2003): 612. JSTOR. Tremough Campus Lib., Penryn. 2nd, August 2009. < http://www.jstor.org/stable/3879463>.

Kranz, David L. "The Sounds of Supernatural Soliciting in "Macbeth"". Studies in Philology. 100 (2003): 350. JSTOR. Tremough Campus Lib., Penryn. 11th, Oct. 2009. <http//:www.jstor.org/stable/4174762>.

Larner. Christina. "Was Witch-Hunting Women-Hunting?" in Darren Oldridge, The Witch Reader. London, New York: Routledge, 2002. pp (273-6).

Levin, Joanna. "Lady Macbeth and the Daemonologie of Hysteria". ELH. 69 (2002): 38. JSTOR. Tremough Campus Lib., Penryn. 18th August. 2009. <http//:www.jstor.org/stable/30032010>.

Lyons, Diane. "Witchcraft, Gender, Power and Intimate Relations in Mura Compounds in Dela, Northern Cameroon". World Archaeology. 29 (1998): (344-345). JSTOR. Tremough Campus Lib., Penryn. 13th October 2009. < http://www.jstor.org/stable/125035>.

McCullen, Joseph T. "Dr Faustus and Renaissance Learning". The Modern Language Review. 51 (1956): (7, 10-11, 13-14). JSTOR. Tremough Campus Lib., Penryn. 26th, August 2009. < http://www.jstor.org/stable/3718255>.

Moran, Gerald F. Rev. of "The Devil's Dominion: Magic and Religion in Early New England" ed. By Richard Godbeer. The Journal of American History. 81 (1994):646. JSTOR. Tremough Campus Lib., Penryn. 2nd, August 2009. < http://www.jstor.org/stable/2081204>.

Muir, Kenneth. The Arden Shakespeare: Macbeth. London: Methuen & Co. Ltd., 1951. Murray, M. A. "A Male Witch and His Familiar". Folklore. 63 (1952): 227. JSTOR. Tremough Campus Lib., Penryn. 13th September 2009. < http://www.jstor.org/stable/1257110>.

Nosworthy, J. M. "The Hecate Scenes in Macbeth Macbeth III. v; IV. I". The Review of English Studies. 24 (1948): 138. JSTOR. Tremough Campus Lib., Penryn. 17th September 2009. < http://www.jstor.org/stable/509937>.

Oldridge, Darren. The Witchcraft Reader. London and New York: Routledge, 2002. Ornstein, Robert. "Marlowe and God: The Tragic Theology of Dr. Faustus". PMLA. 83 (1968): (1380, 1382). JSTOR. Tremough Campus Lib., Penryn. 26th, August 2009. < http://www.jstor.org/stable/1261310>.

Purkiss, Diana. The Witch in History: Early Modern and twentieth-Century Representations. London and New York: Routledge, 1996. Rosen, Barbara. Witchcraft in England, 1558- 1618. New York: The University of Massachusetts Press Amherst, 1991.

Rosenthal, Bermard. Rev. of "Witchcraft, Magic, and Religion in Seventeenth-Century Massachusetts" ed. By Richard Weisman. The New England Quarterly. 57 (1984): (598, 600). JSTOR. Tremough Campus Lib., Penryn. 2nd, August 2009. <http://www. jstor.org/stable/365068>

Salih, Sara. "Judith Butler". London and New York: Routledge, Google Book. 2002.<http://books.google. co.uk/books?id=Eb7WiUfQ9AoC&pg=PP1&source =gbs selected pages&cad=0 1#PPA104,M1>.pp. (90-1, 104).

Sawyer, Ronald C. "'Strangely Handled in All Her Lyms': Witchcraft and Healing in Jacobean England". Journal of Social History. 22 (1989): (461, 465). JSTOR. Tremough Campus Lib., Penryn. 2nd, August 2009. < http://www.jstor.org/stable/3787745>.

Schafer, Elizabeth. The Witch: Thomas Middleton. London and New York: A and c Black,1994. Schick, Mary. "Magic". The American Journal of Nursing. 29 (1929): 1075. JSTOR. Tremough

Campus Lib., Penryn. 6th, August 2009. <http://www.jstor.org/stable/3410131>.

Schoenbaum, Samuel. "Middleton's Tragicomedies". Modern Philology. 54 (1956): 9. JSTOR. Tremough Campus Lib., Penryn. 13th September 2009. < http://www.jstor.org/stable/435153>.

Showalter, Elaine. "Feminist Criticism in the Wilderness". Critical Inquiry. 8 (1981): 187. JSTOR. Tremough Campus Lib., Penryn. 10th October 2009. <http://www.jstor.org/stable/1343159>

Simpson, Jacqueline. "Witches and Witchbusters". Folklore. 107 (1996): (5-8, 10, 12). JSTOR. Tremough Campus Lib., Penryn. 2nd, August 2009. <http://www.jstor.org/stable/1260910>.

Tate, William. "Solomon, Gender, and Empire in Marlowe's Doctor Faustus". Studies in English Literature. 37 (1997): 267. JSTOR. Tremough Campus Lib., Penryn. 26th, August 2009. < http://www.jstor.org/stable/450833>.

Thompson, Roger. Rev. of "Witchcraft, Magic, and Religion in the 17th century Massachusetts". Ed. By Richard Weisman. Journal of American Studies. 20 (1986): 308. JSTOR. Tremough Campus Lib., Penryn. 2nd, August 2009. < http://www.jstor.org/stable/27554772>.

Tolman, Albert H. "Notes on Macbeth". PMLA. 2 (1896): (208, 211-212). JSTOR. Tremough Campus Lib., Penryn. 6th, August 2009. <http//:www.jastor.org/stable/456259>.

Walker, William H. "Where are the Witches of Prehistory". Journal of Archaeological Method and Theory. 5 (1998):. JSTOR. Tremough Campus Lib., Penryn. 12th, October 2009. < http://www.jstor.org/stable/20177387>

Willis, Deborah. Malevolent Nurture: Witch Hunting and Maternal Power in Early Modern England. Ithaca and London: Cornell University Press, 1995.